AF581251

CAT DAYS

Photographs
by

TORAHIKO YAMASHITA

CAT DAYS

Photographed by Torahiko Yamashita ©
Published by Graphic-sha Publishing Company Ltd.©

First Edition September 1990
ISBN4-7661-0573-7

Graphic-sha Publishing Company Ltd.
1-9-12 Kudan-kita Chiyoda-ku Tokyo 102 Japan
Phone 03-263-4318
Fax 03-263-5297
Telex J29877 Graphic

Printed in Japan by Toppan Printing Co., Ltd.

CAT DAYS
猫

山下寅彦写真集

［エッセー］

英語翻訳
エイドリアン·J·ピニングトン

ESSAYS

English Translation by
Adrian J. Pinnington

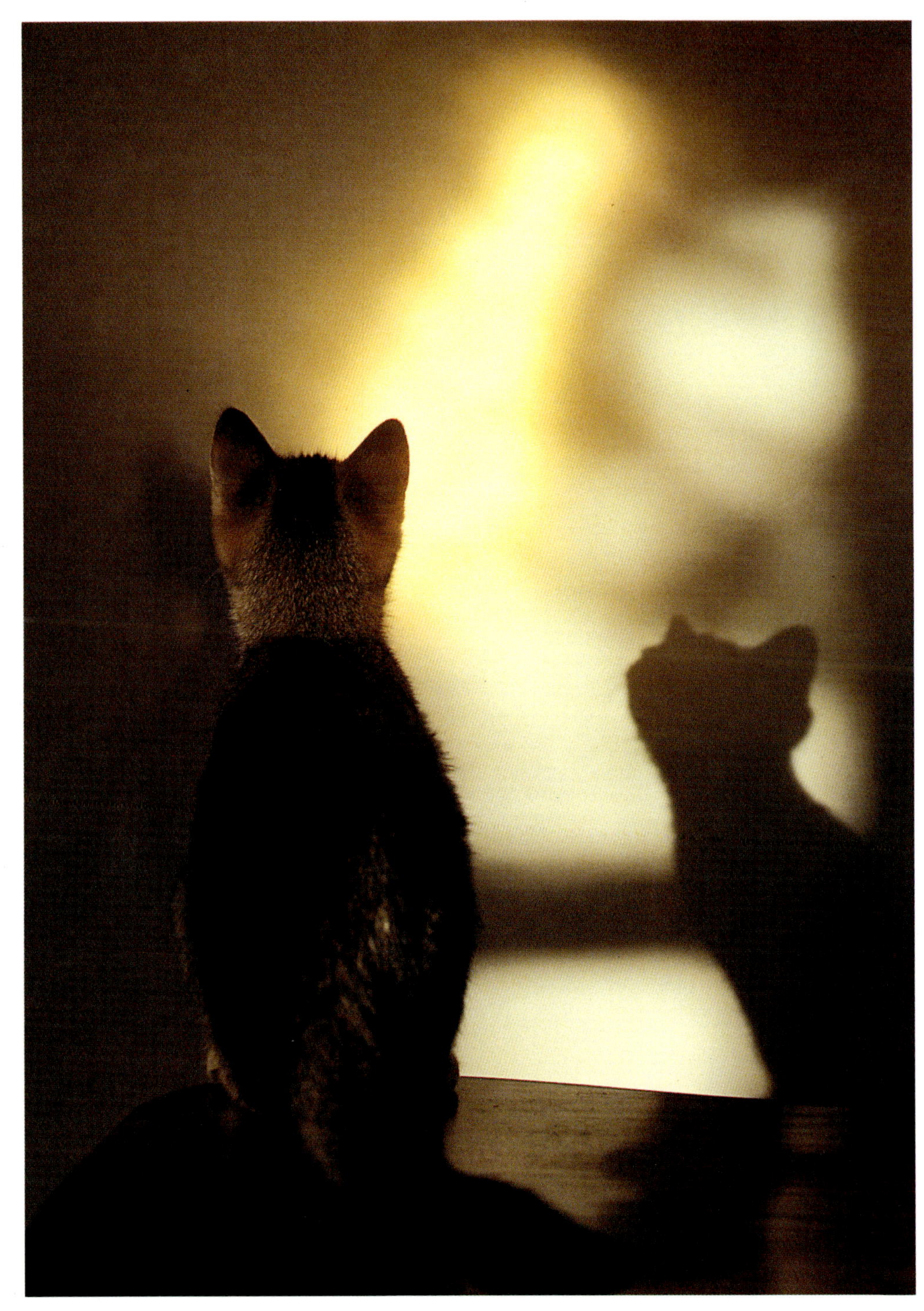

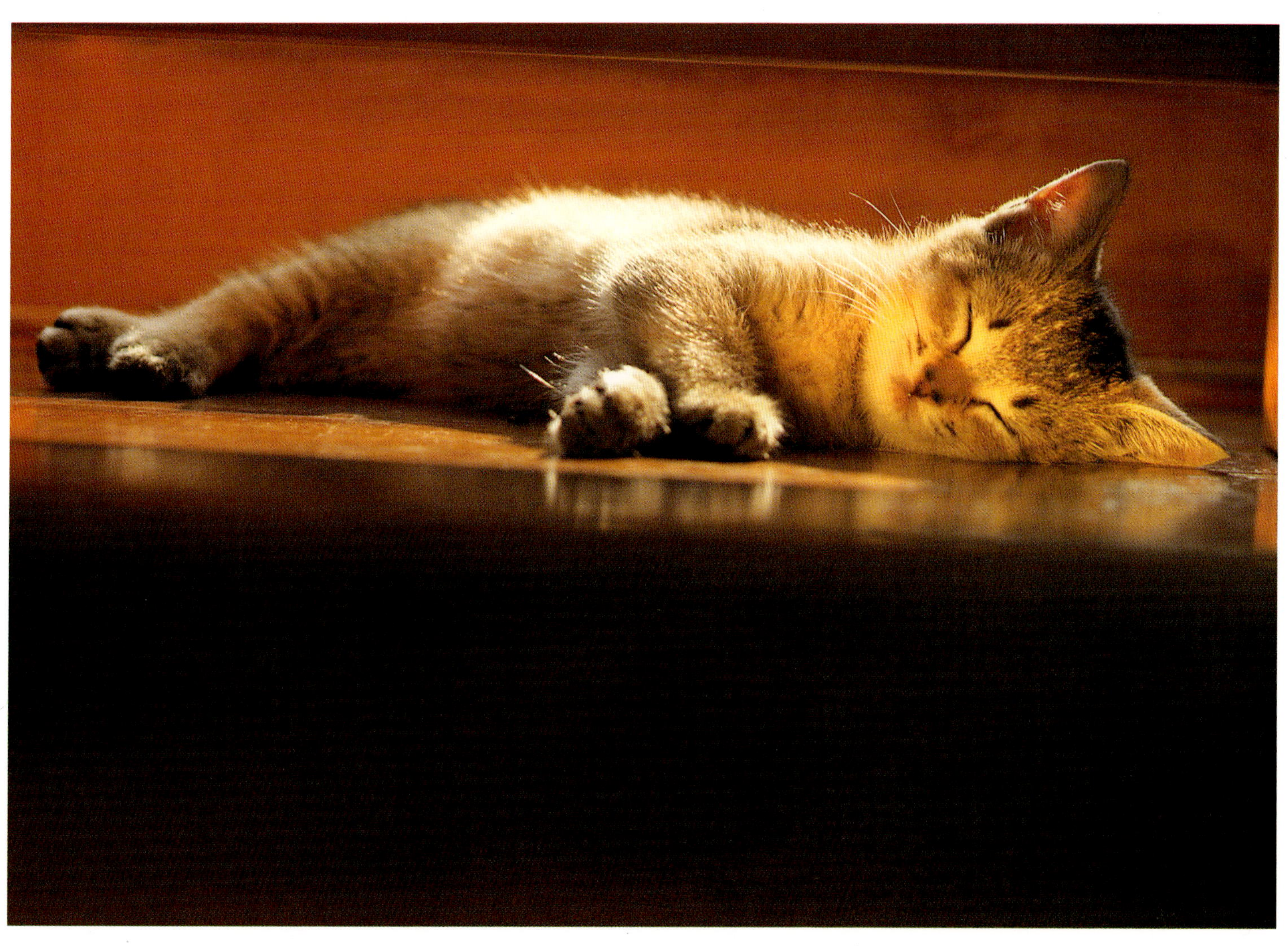

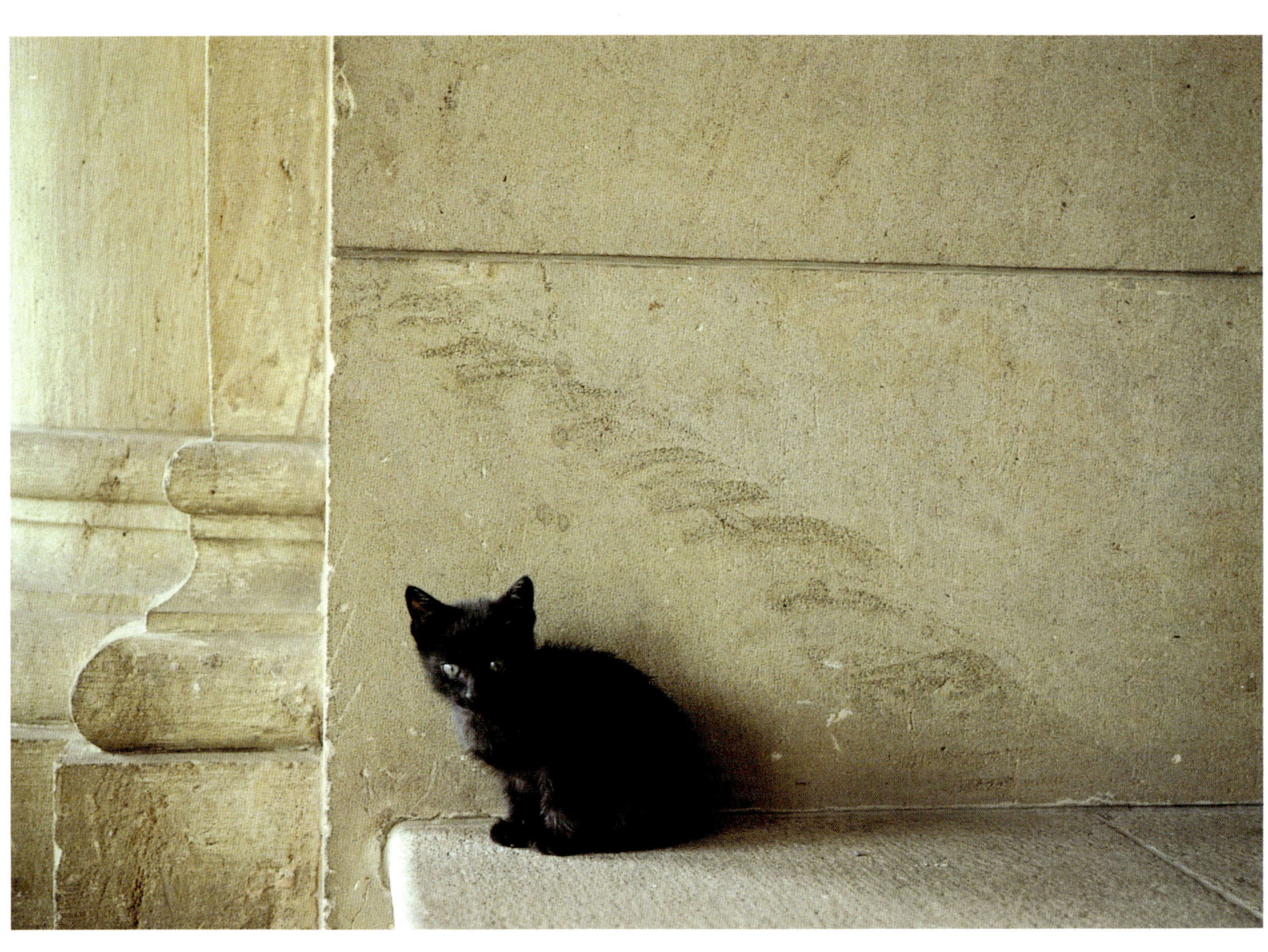

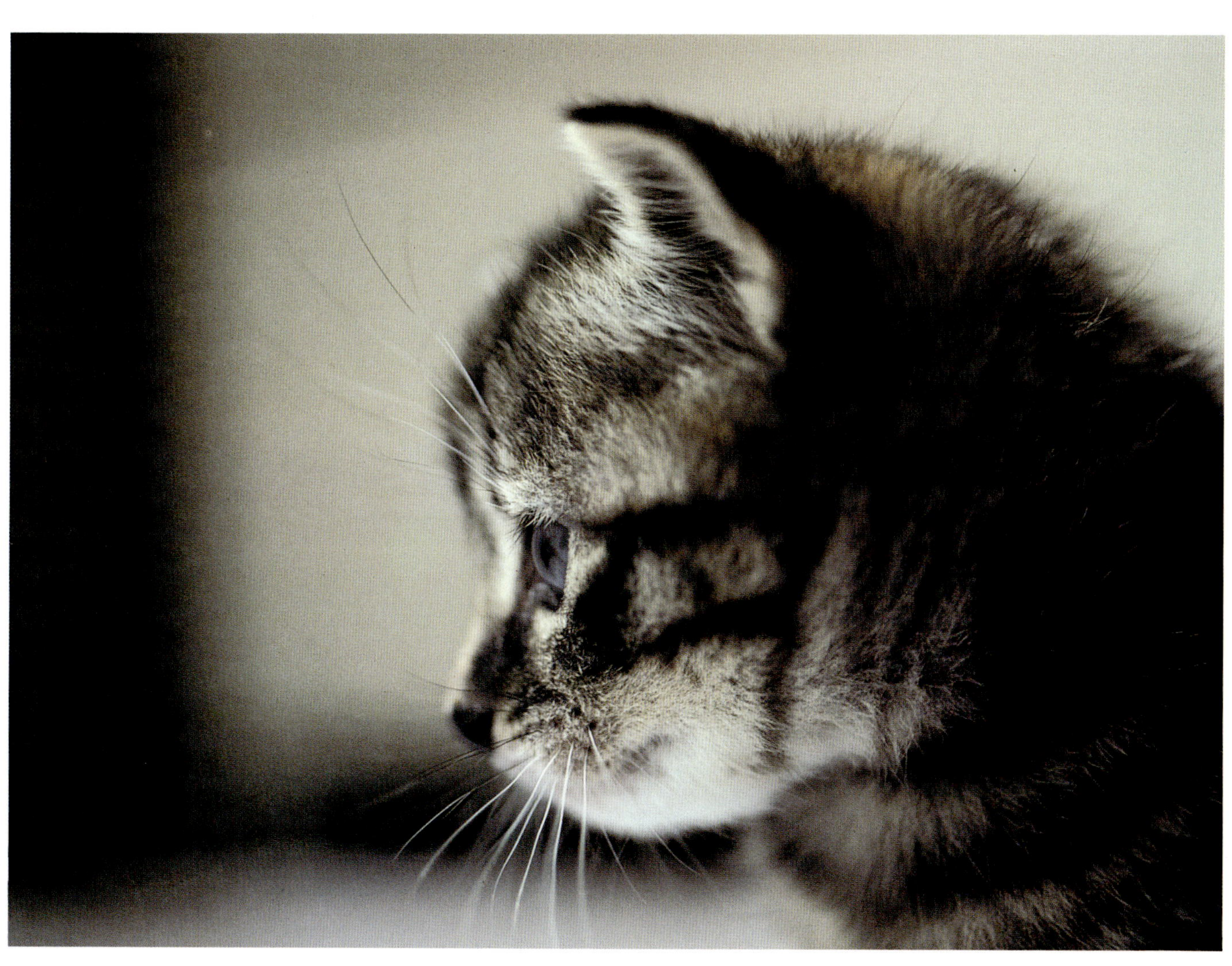

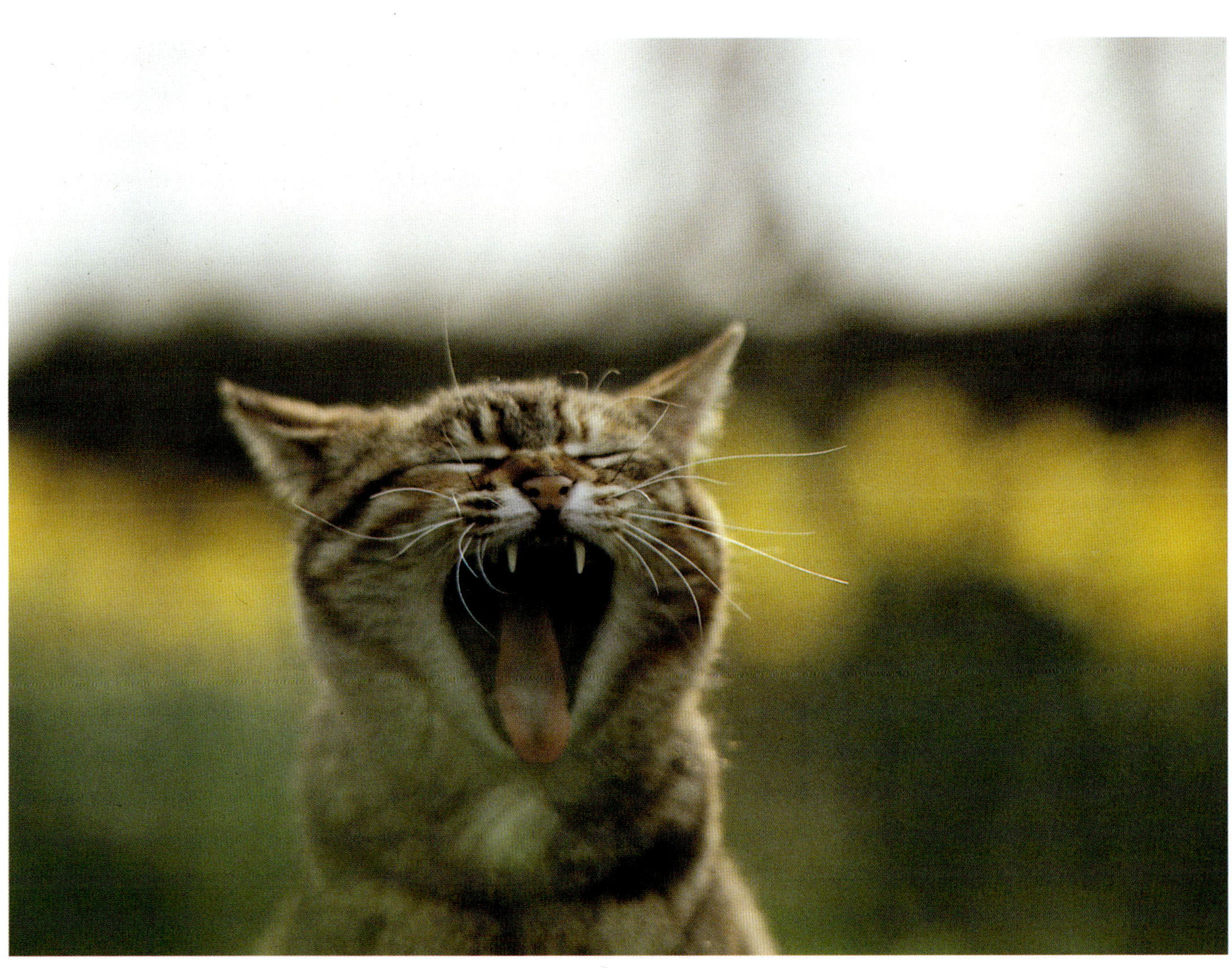

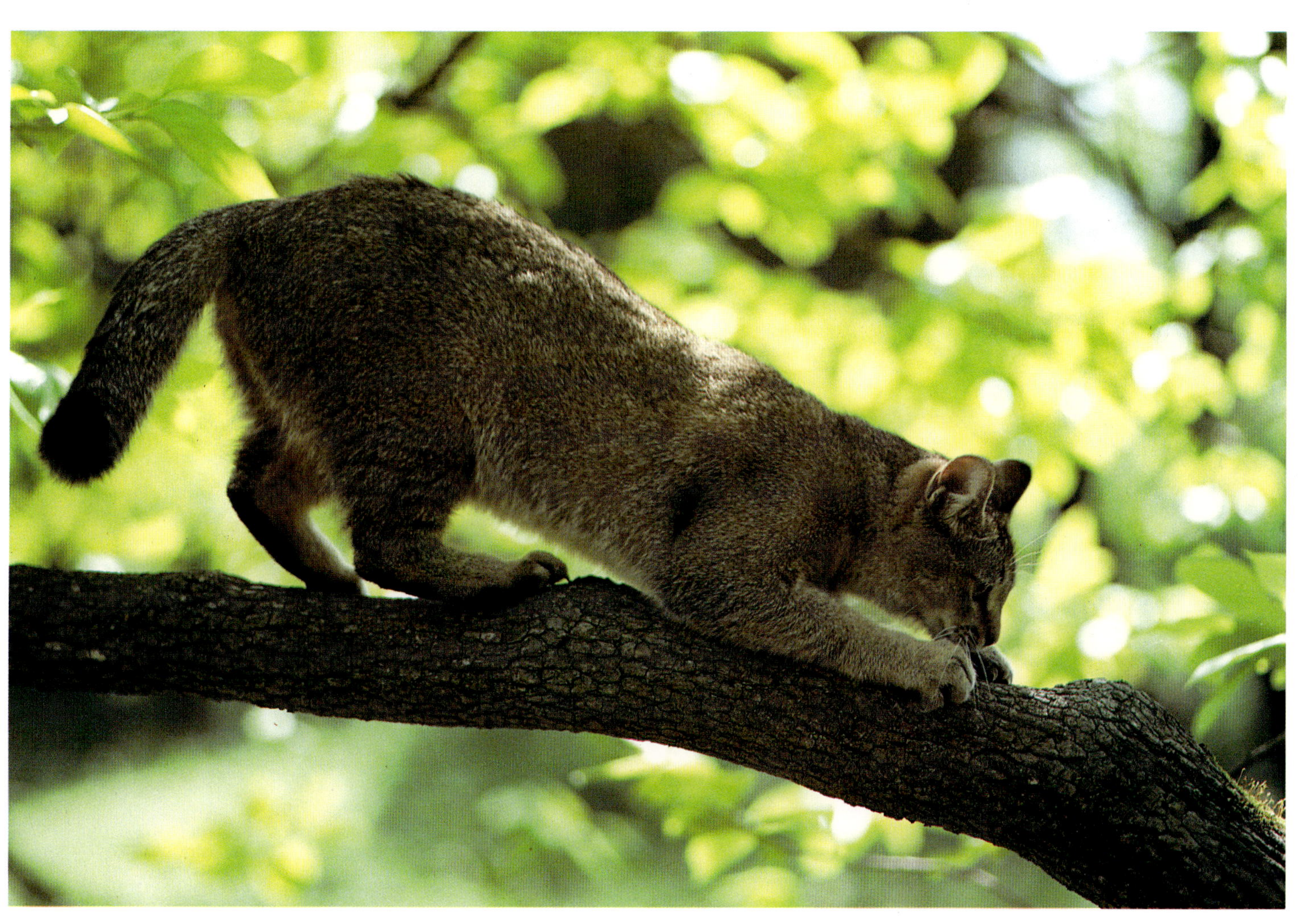

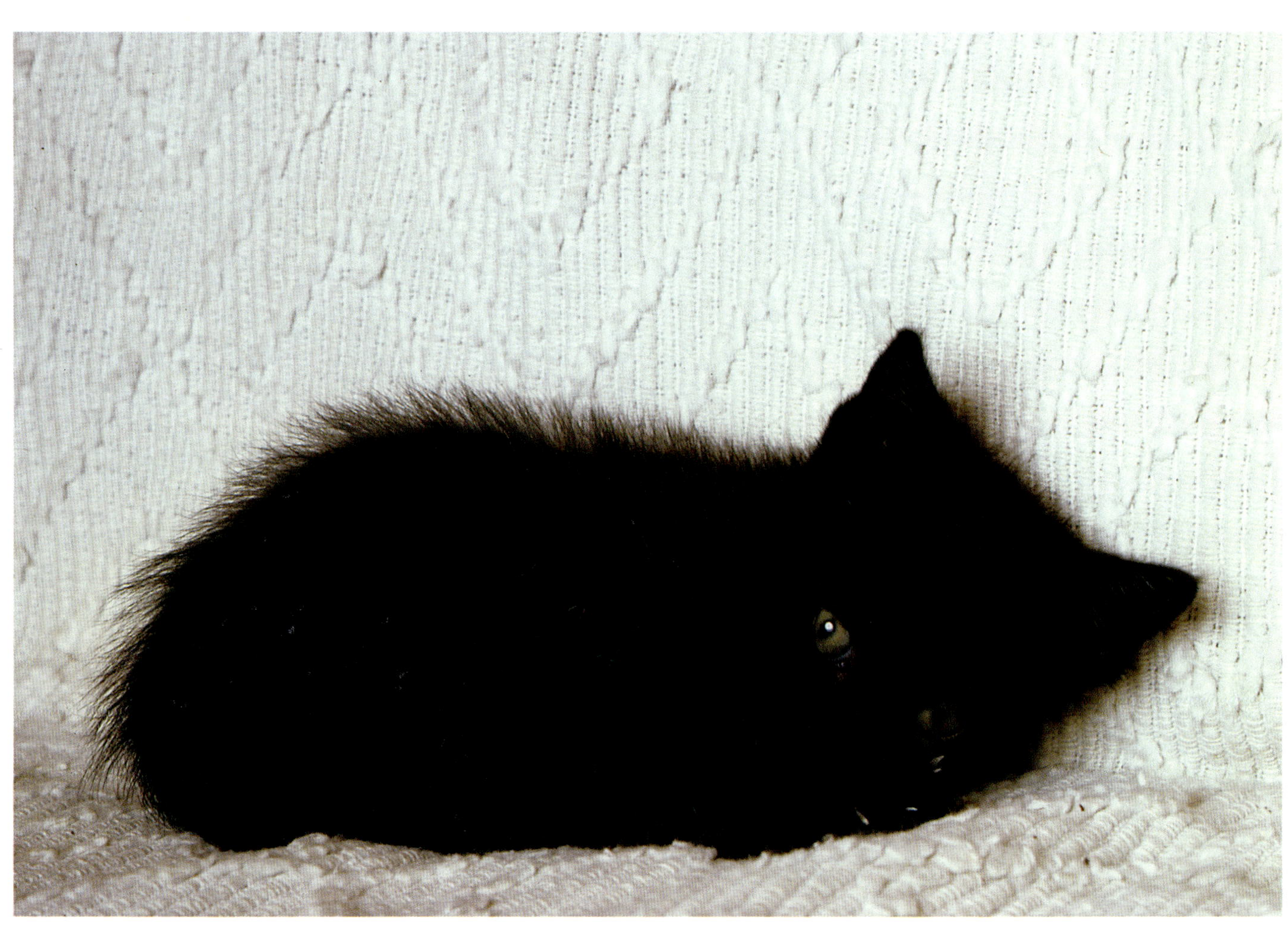

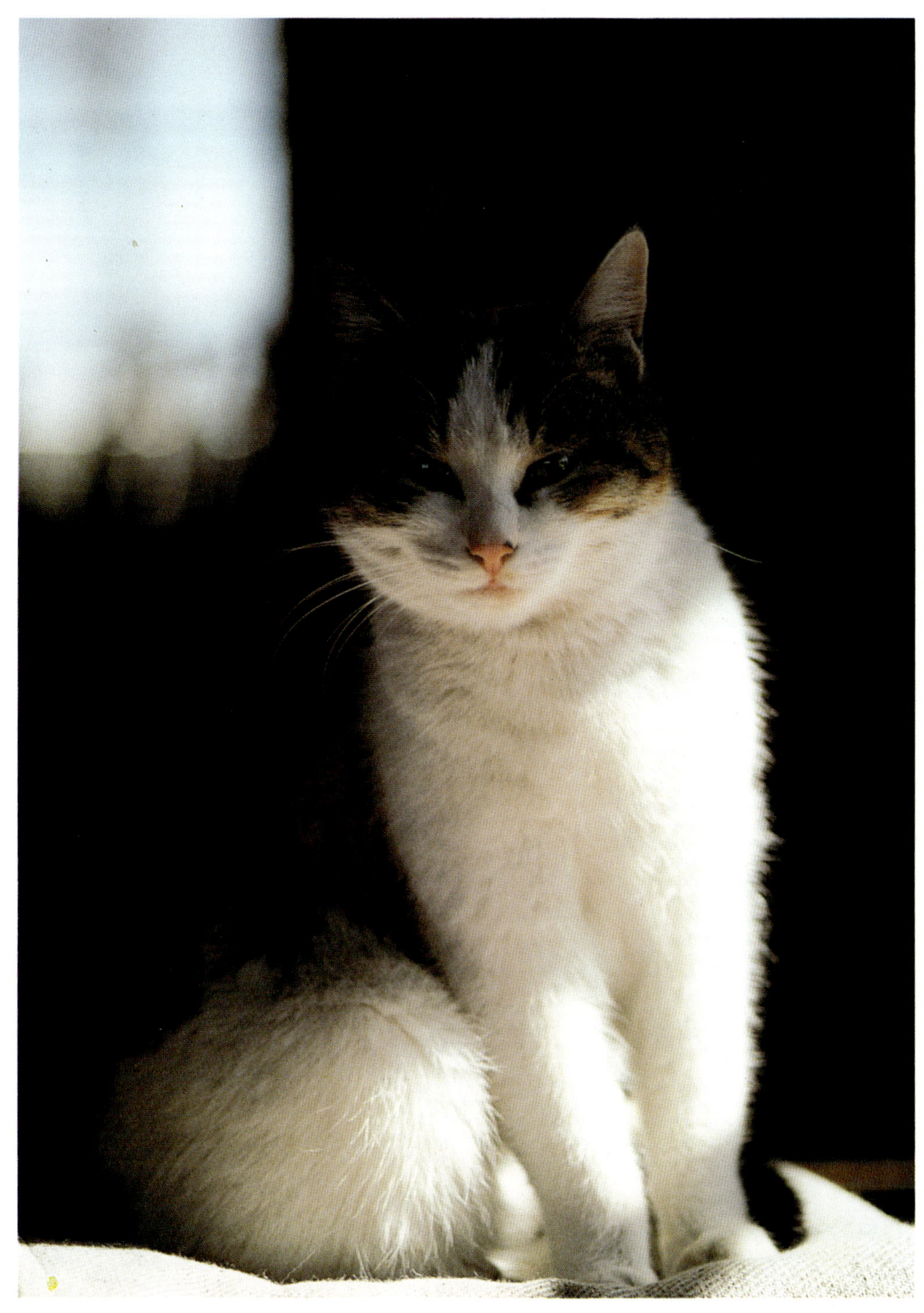

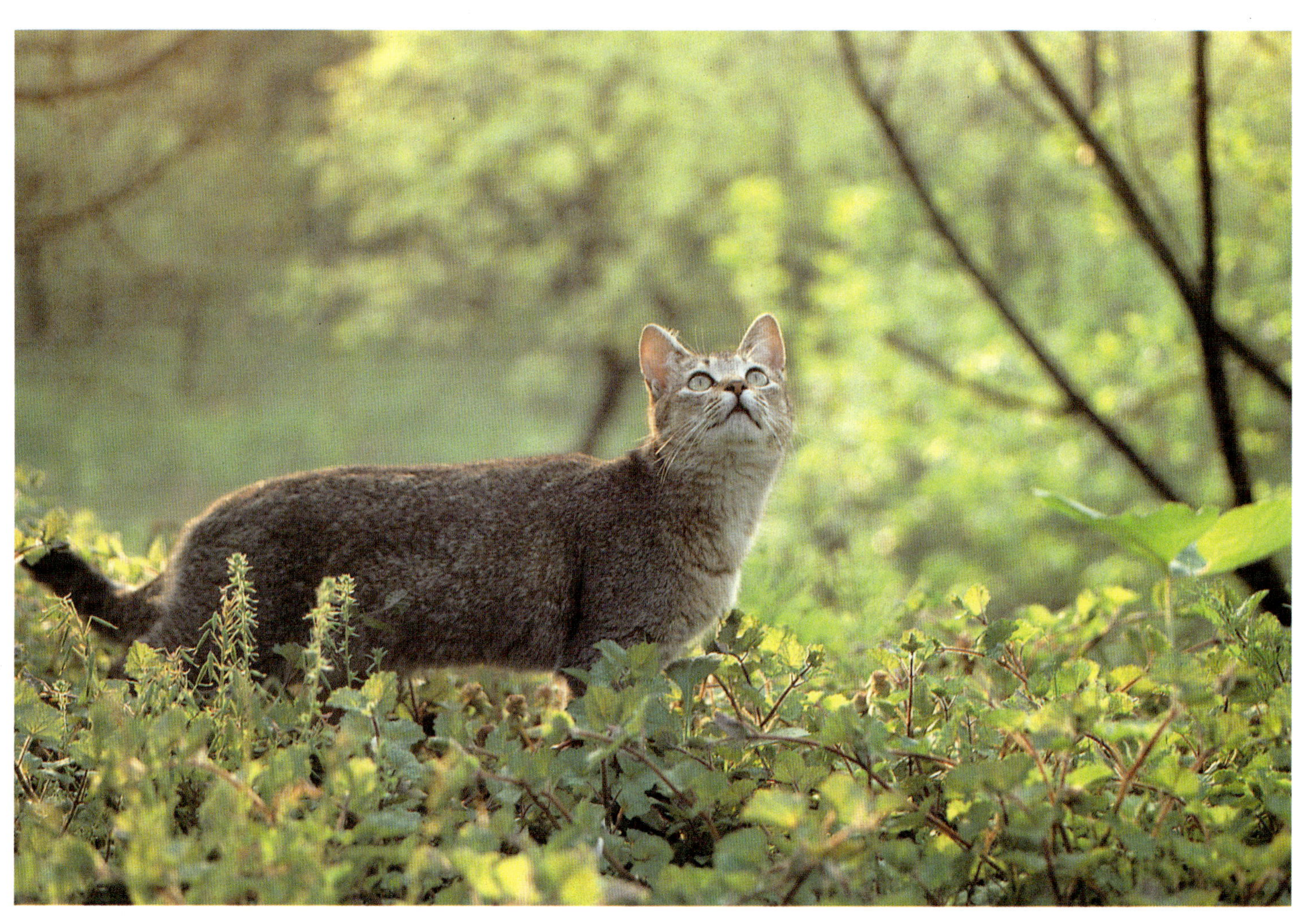

対話

日高敏隆
動物学者

猫は何を考えているのだろう？

テレビの上や戸棚の上。思いおもいの小さな場所にじっと坐って，どこかをみつめるともなくみつめている。前肢をすっとそろえ，尾をくるりと後肢のわきにまわした姿は，うらやましいほど美しい置き物だ。

でもこの置き物は，きっと何かを考えている。そうでなかったら，あんな真面目な顔をして，いつまでもじっとしているはずがない。

お前，何を考えているの？

そう聞いてみたい気持は山々だけど，聞いてみたって，答えてくれるはずはない。でも，やっぱり思いきって聞いてみようか。いややめよう，でもやっぱり。

決心して，ぼくは声をかける。

お前，何を考えているの？

猫は首を少し傾けて，椅子に坐ったぼくを見る。小声でニャアともいわないで。そのときの猫のけげんそうな顔。それはまさに，この人，何を考えているのだろう？　という顔だ。

お前はぼくが何を考えているのか知りたいんだね。ぼくはお前が何を考えているかを知りたいんだ。

けれど，どちらからも答えはない。猫はぼくに問い，ぼくは猫に問う。こうして何秒かの沈黙がつづく。ほんの短い間だけど，この沈黙は耐えがたい。ぼくは顔をそっと転じて，庭先を見る。

ほんのたった１，２秒。ぼくはまた猫のほうへ視線を戻す。そして，今そこにいた猫の姿が，早やどこかへ消えてしまっていることを発見する。

Dialogue

Toshitaka Hidaka
Zoologist

What do cats think about ?

On top of the television or on top of a cupboard, each in its own favourite little place, cats sit unmoving, gazing at nothing in particular. With their front paws neatly arranged, their tails smoothly curled around the back paws, they look like beautiful ornaments.

Yet this ornament is surely thinking about something. If not, it would not sit unmoving for so long with such a serious face.

What are you thinking about ?

This is what I really feel like asking. But even if I ask, the cat won't reply. Still, I'll have a go and ask. No, no, there's no point. Still...

Finally I make up my mind and speak out.

"What are you thinking about ?"

The cat bends its neck a little and looks at me sitting in my chair. She doesn't give even the slightest miaow in reply. But what a puzzled expression a cat wears at such a time, as if to say "What on earth is this human being thinking about !"

Oh, so you want to know what I am thinking about ? Well, I want to know what you are thinking about.

However, neither of us answers the other. The cat looks enquiringly at me and I at her. For some seconds the silence continues. The silence only lasts a few seconds, but it is difficult to bear. I turn my face away casually and look out at the garden.

It is only one or two seconds before I turn my eyes back to her. But when I do so, I find that the cat, which was here only a moment before, has already vanished.

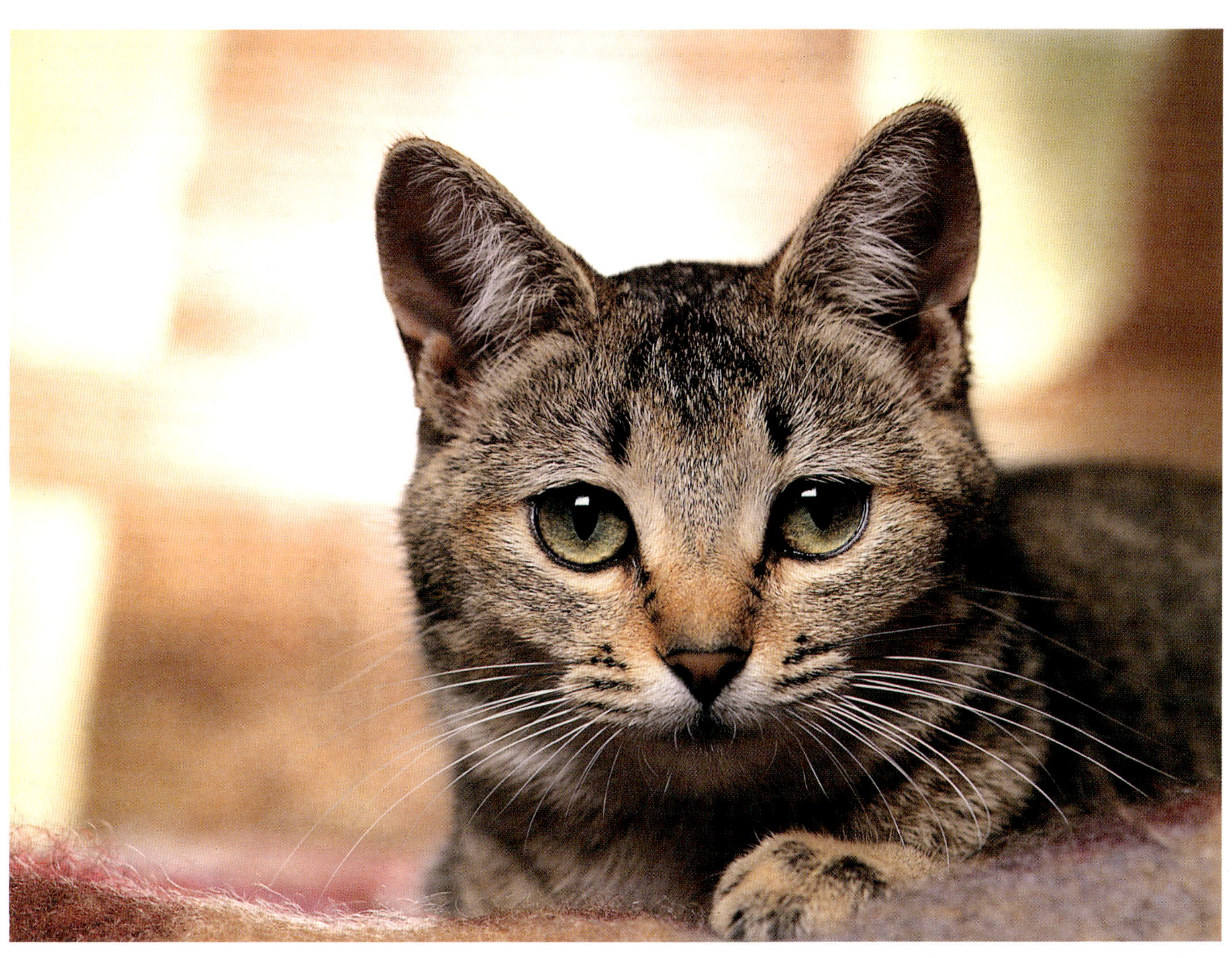

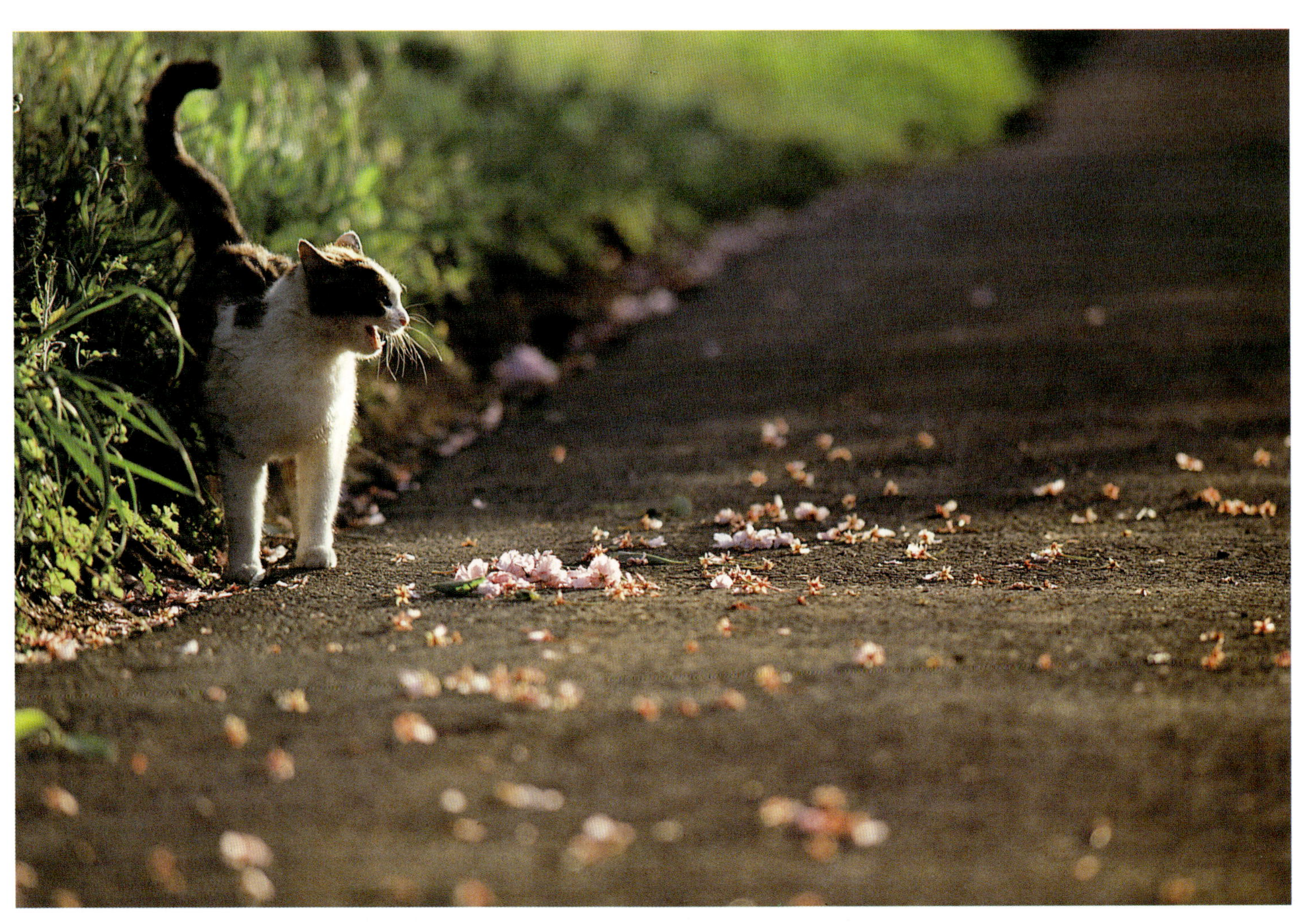

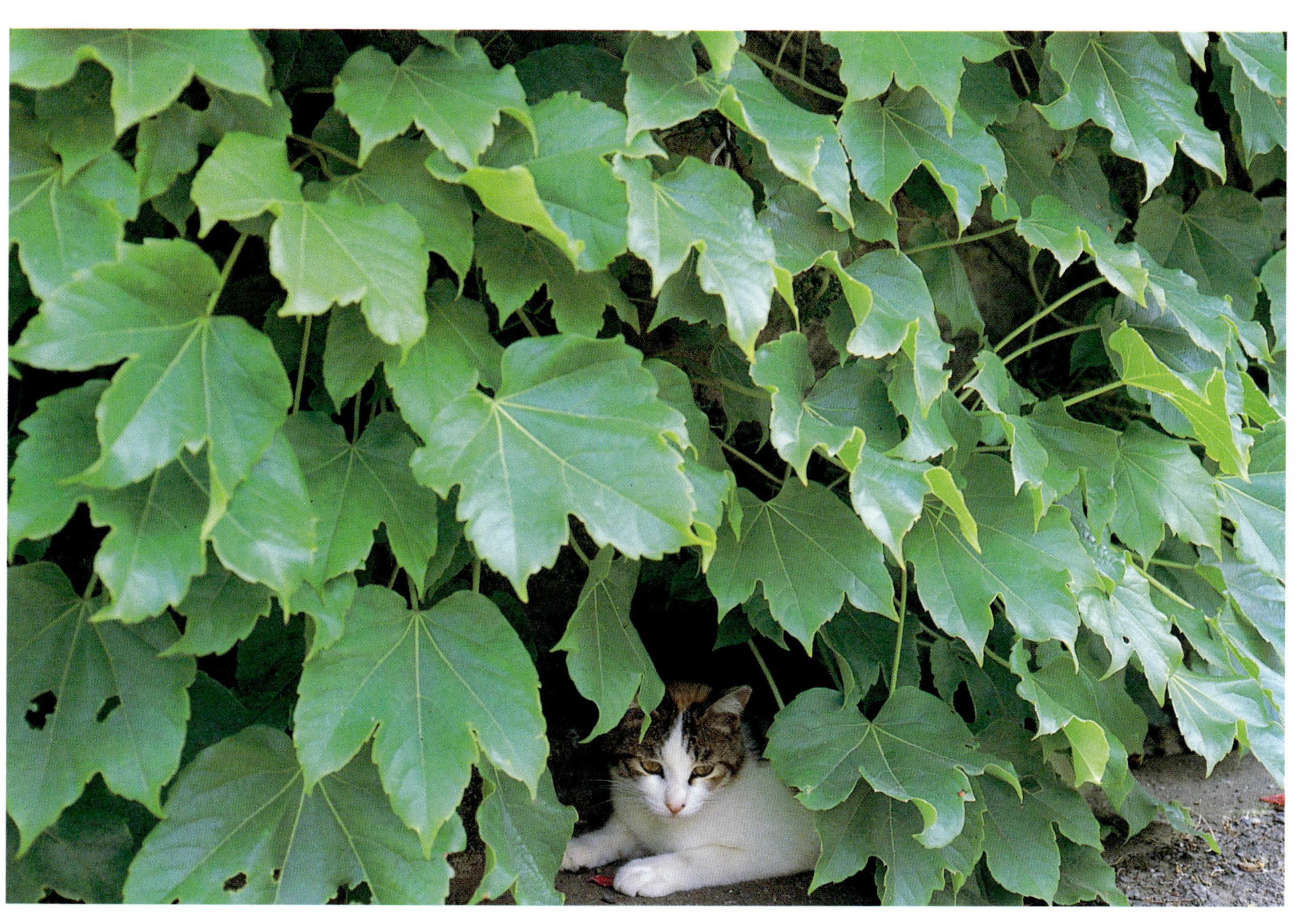

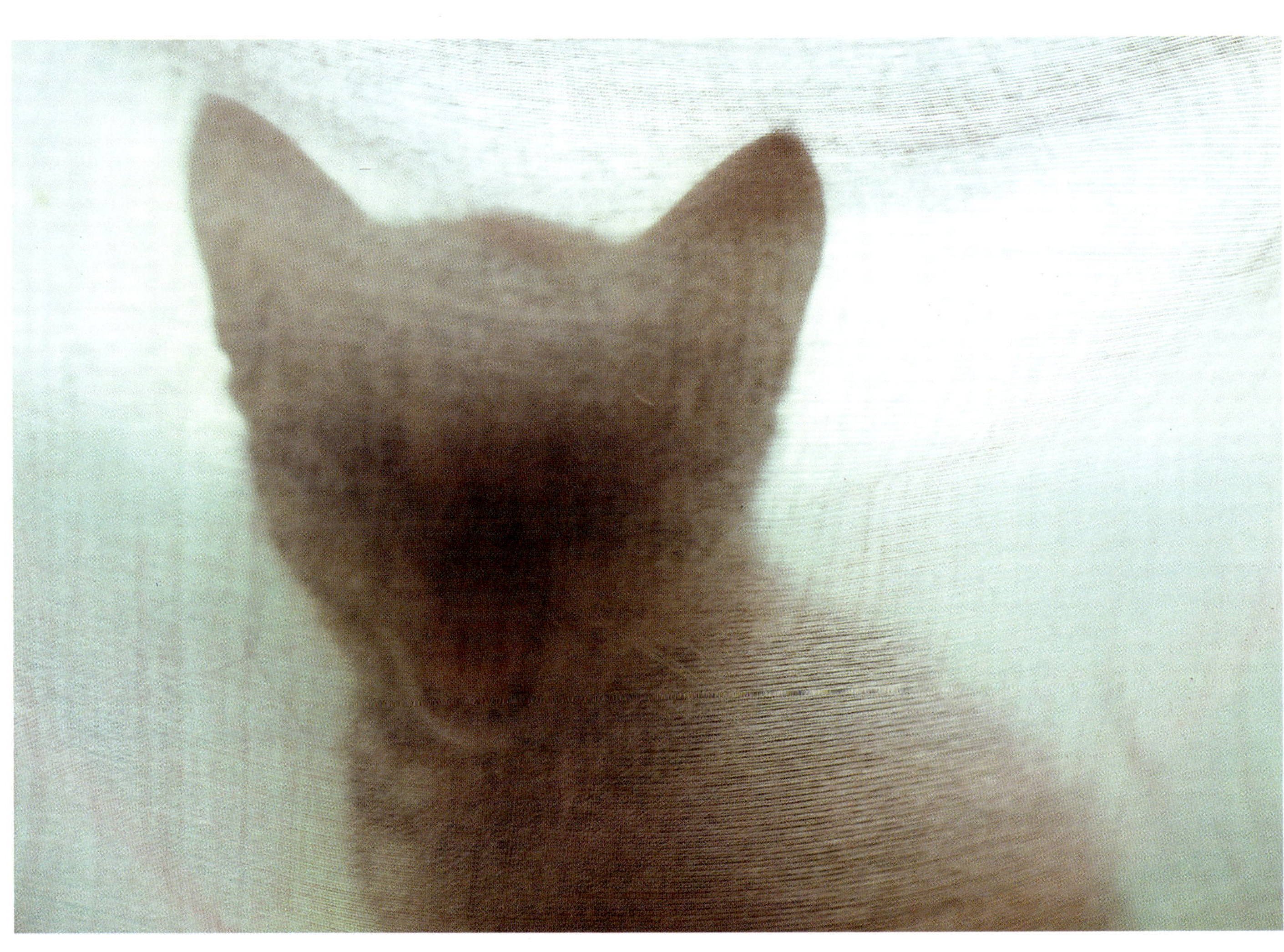

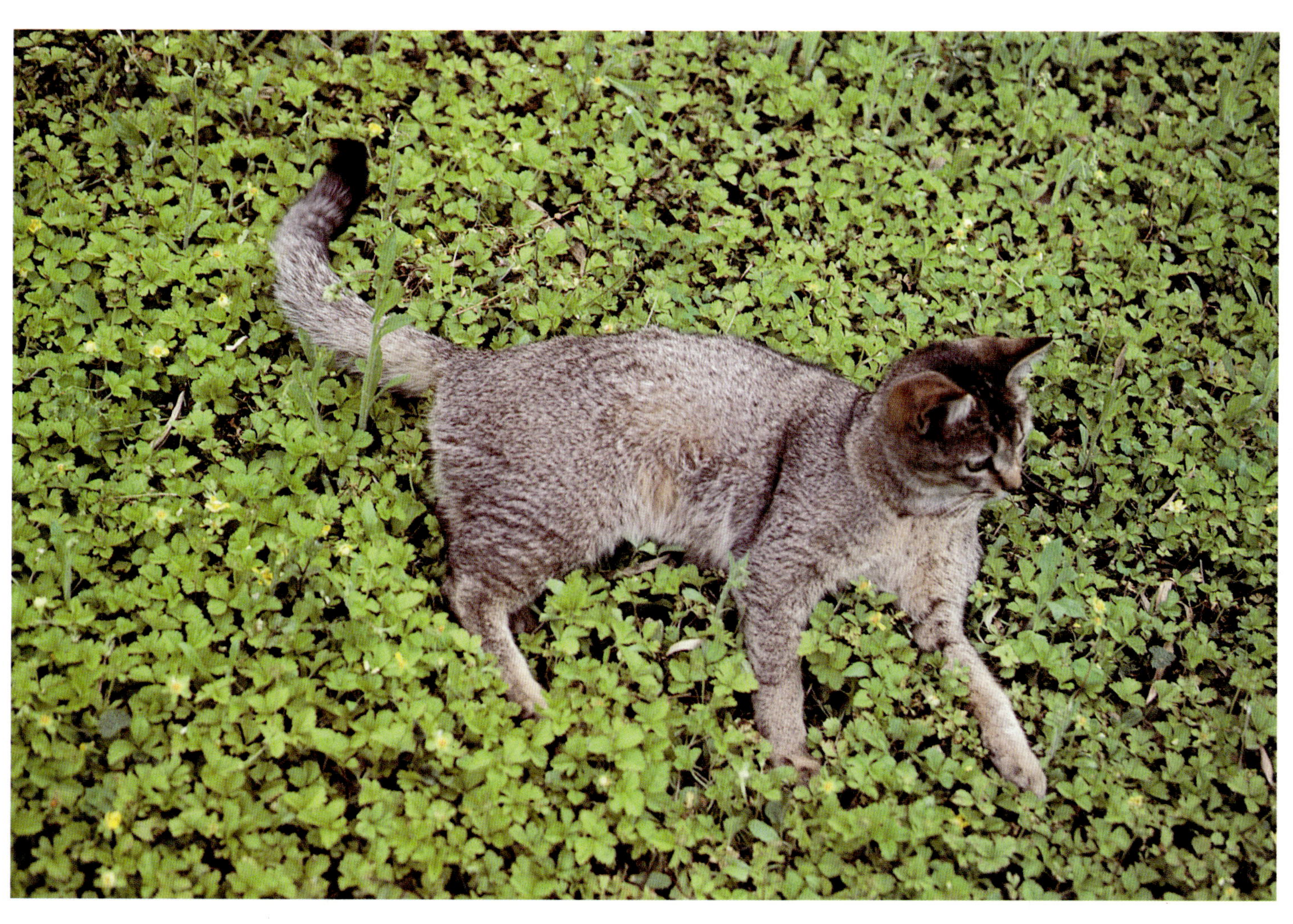

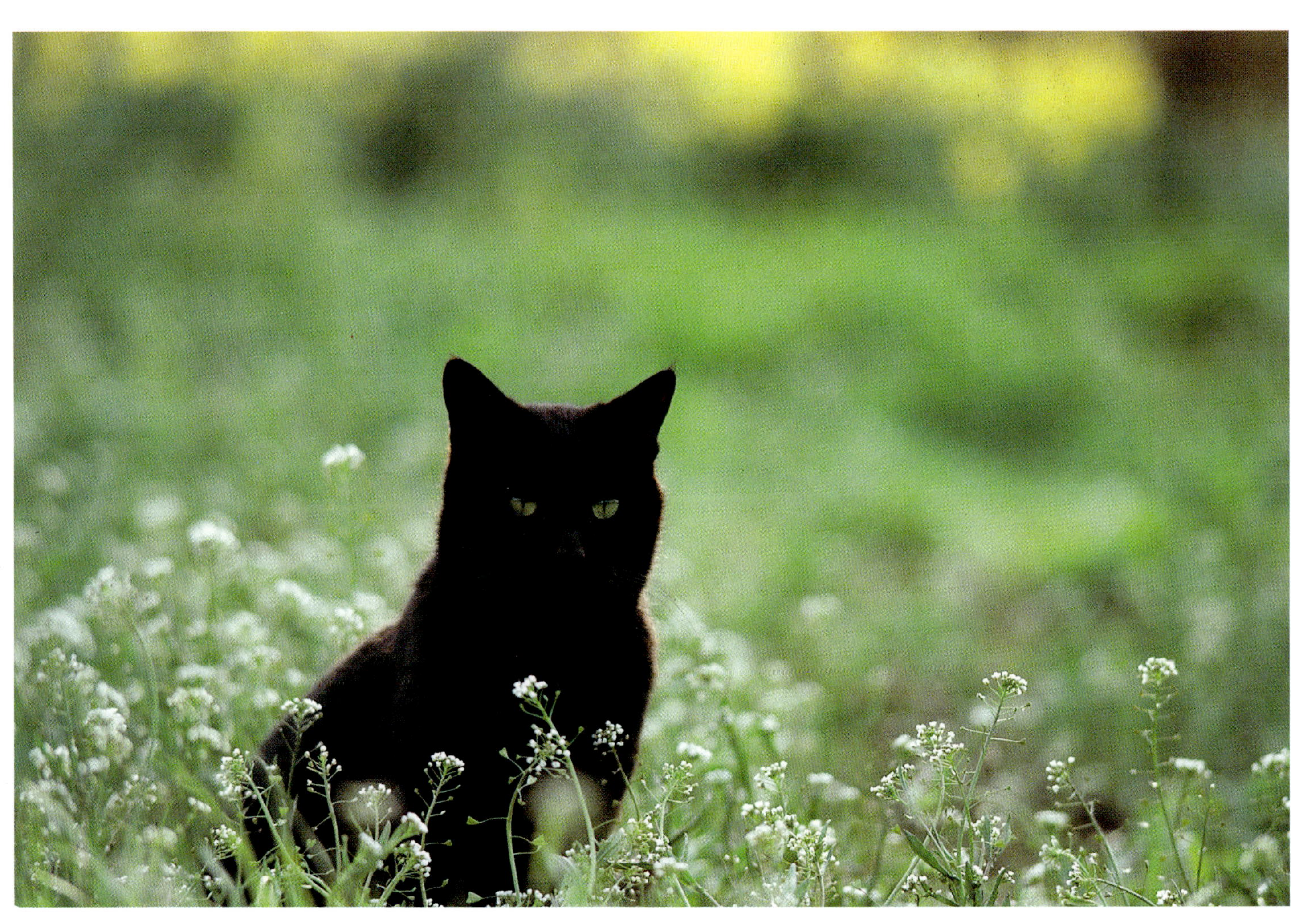

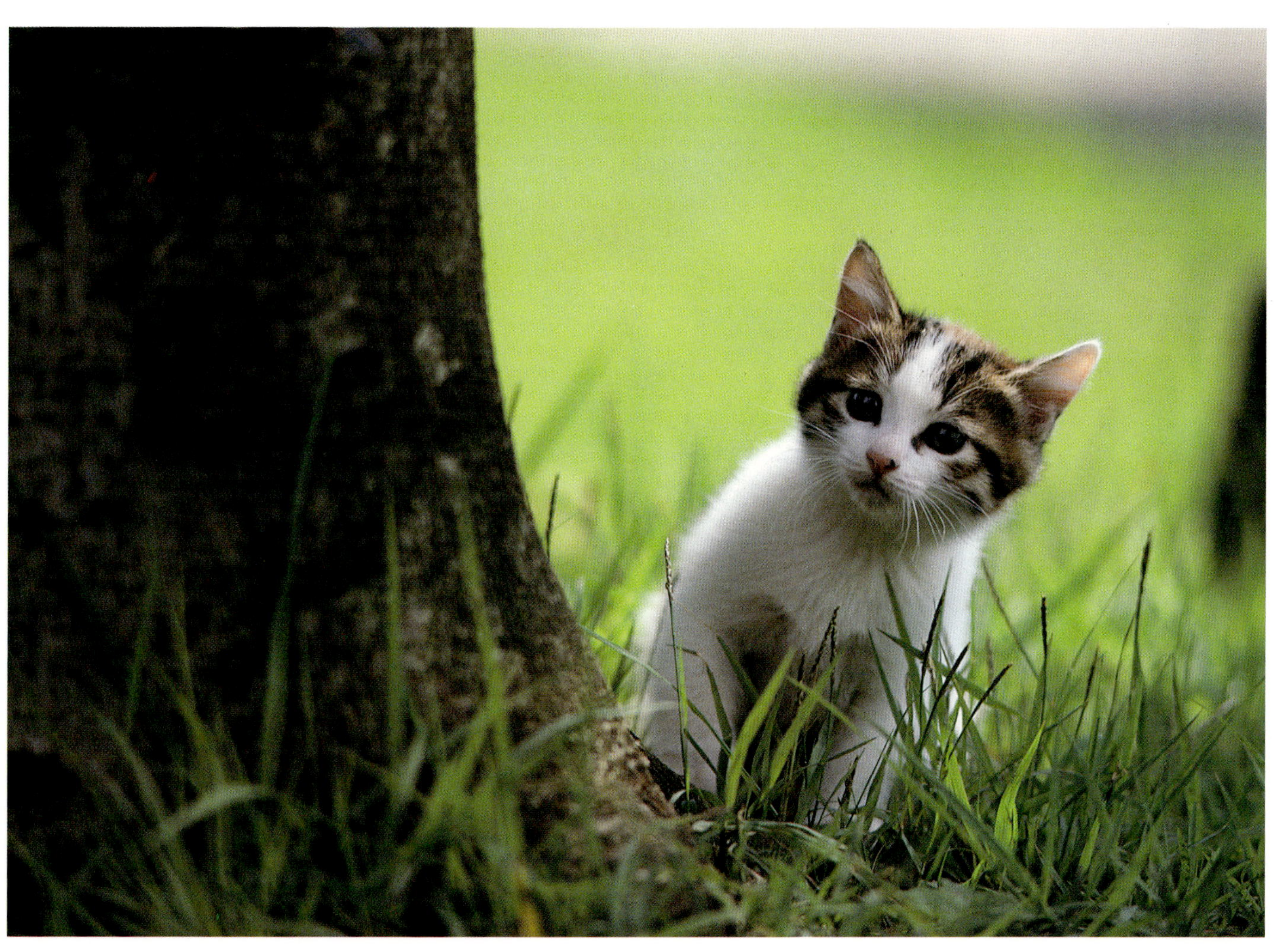

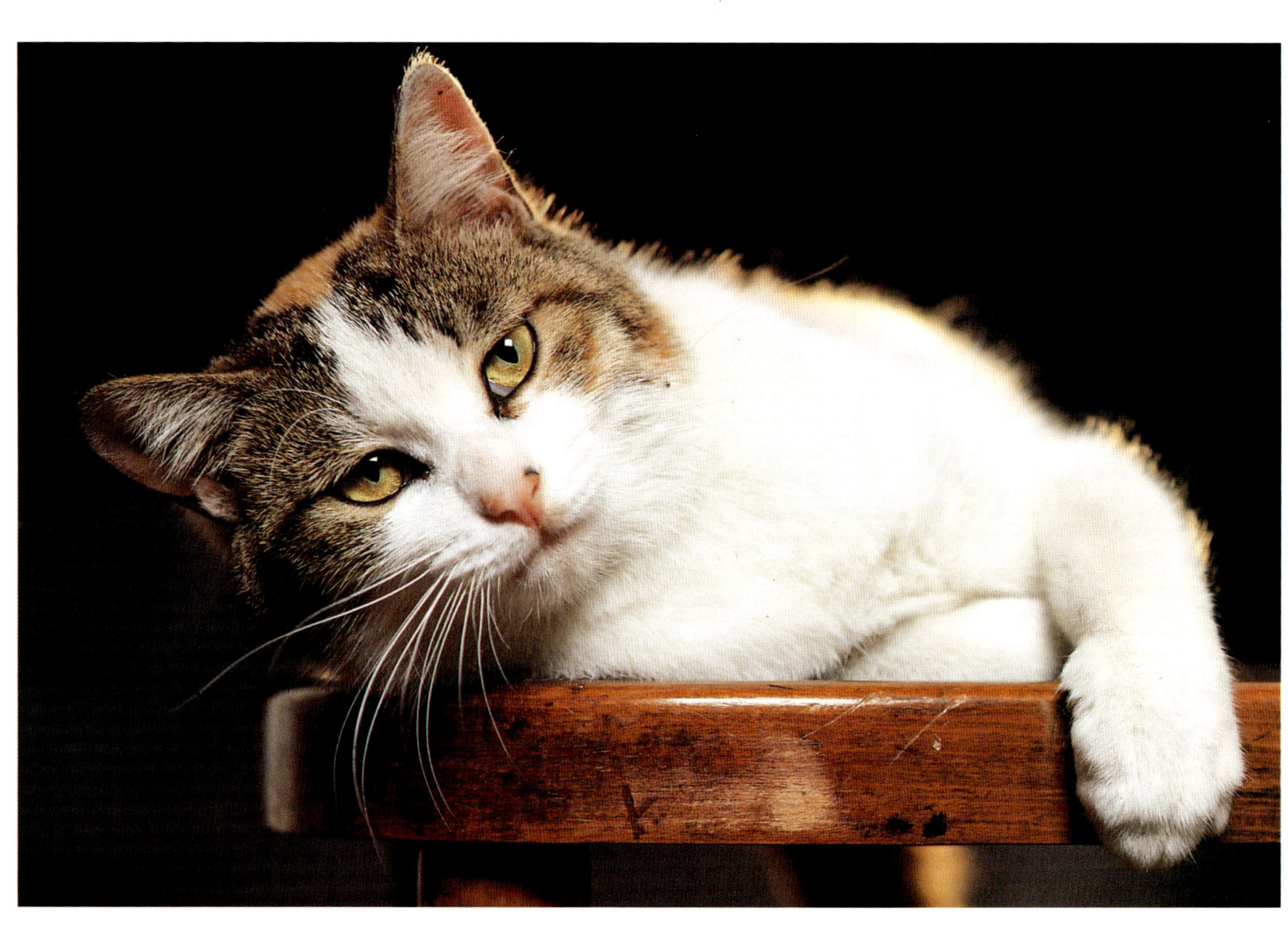

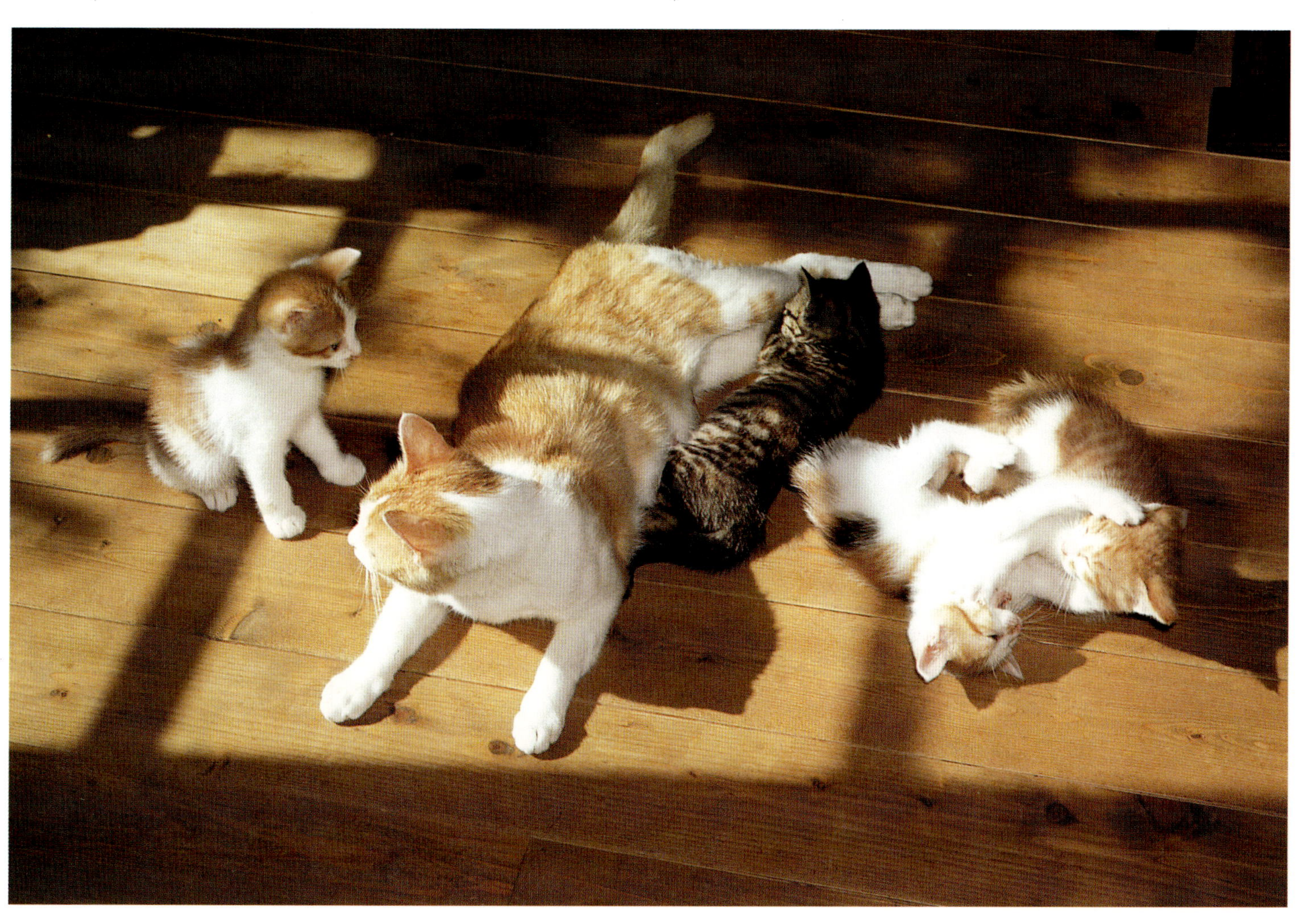

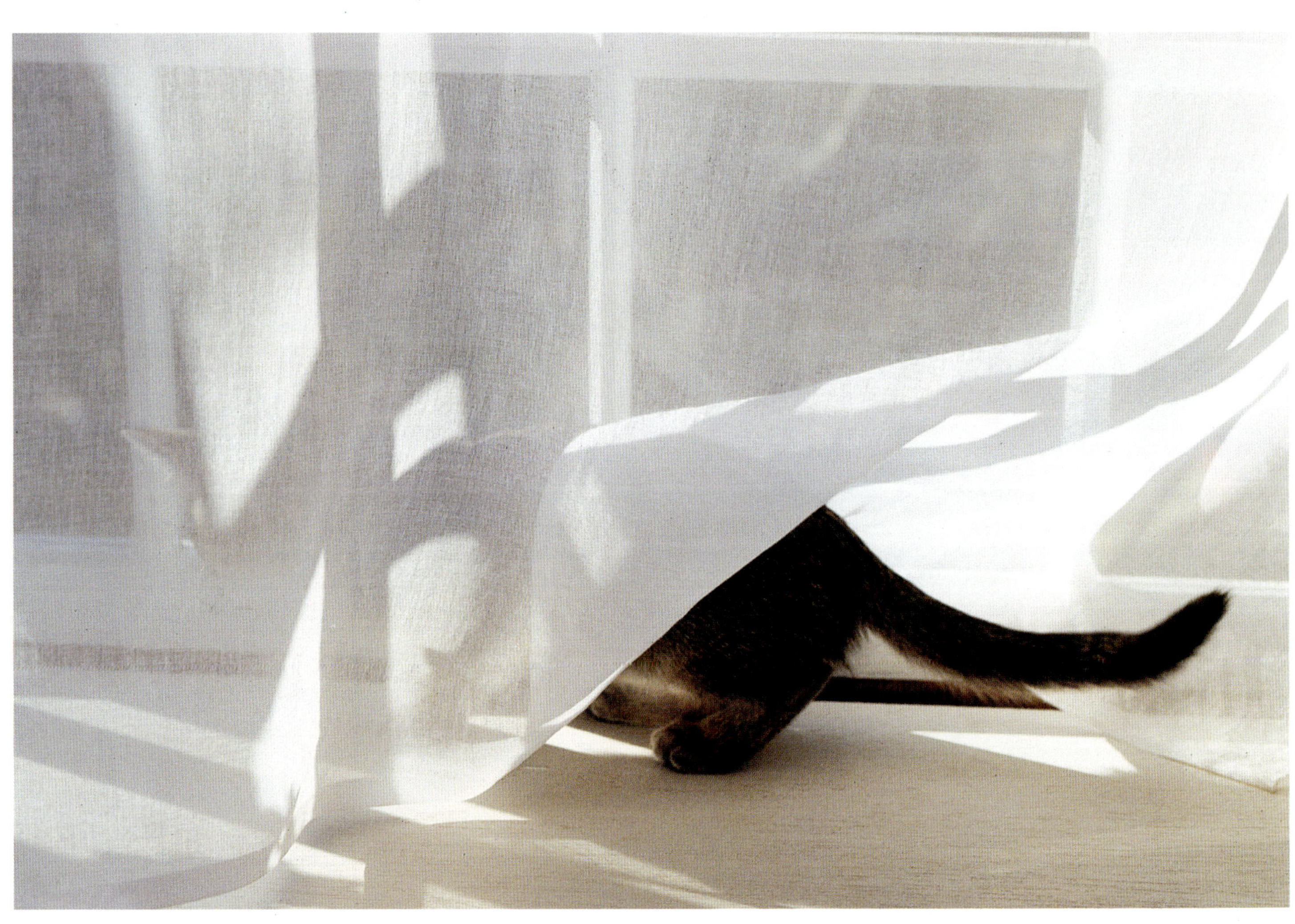

もの云わぬから

佐野洋子
絵本作家

私は小さな家に息子と二人で住んでいた。それから猫が一匹いた。悪さの盛りの息子は，一ヶ月に一度も私にものを問いかけることさえなくて，私は時々遠くを見てボーッと涙をだらだら流していた。大きなガラス戸の向こうの林と空を見て，天気がよかったりすると涙は，ことさらだらだらと流れるのである。

れんぎょうと米桜が，今を盛りと光るベランダを猫がのたのたと横切ると，私は猫って変だなとボーッと見ている。一緒に何年も住んでいて，気が通じているのかいないのか，とにかく一晩も外泊も旅行もせずに，当然のごとく飯を食い好きなところに寝ている。「ありがとうございます」ぐらい云ってもらいたいものだ，「小さい時はあの息子さまにしっぽをふり回されて私も大変な思いをいたしました，でも，大丈夫ですよ，きっと。私もそれで猫が練れました，おかげさまで」と，私の涙をなめてくれてもよさそうなものだ。「きっと立派な男に成長する激動の時代なのですよ」くらい云えるだろ。

しかし猫は生意気っぽく見えるうす目をあけて，ドタリと日あたりのいい床に横たわり一心不乱に自分の腹のあたりをなめ回すばかりである。「何でお前だけが呑気なんだよ」。私は突然腹が立ち，必要もないのに猫をけとばして歩いた。猫はひょいとタンスの上にのっかった。

そして月日は流れて，激動の時代は去った。白目をむいていた少年は，ほれぼれする若者である。そして巣立っていった。しかし，猫はまだ私と一緒に居る。おまけにめっちゃくちゃに愛し合う相手まで出て来てしまった。外は初夏の緑がもえて，開け放した窓から風がさぁーっと吹き抜けていく。私達は，並んで外を見ている。私達より幸せの人が世の中に居たら変と思わない？

その時猫が，静かに歩いて来て，私達の間にまるまった。私達は「ふふふ」とものすごくやさしい笑い声が出て来て，二人で猫をなでた。いい子だね，猫って，もの云わないから完璧なんだ。お前がいまここにいるから私達も完璧になっちゃった。ふふふ。いい子だね。

Cats Never Say Anything

Yoko Sano
Children's Author

I used to live in a small house with just my son. And one cat.

My son was in his worst phase. Sometimes he didn't even address a question to me for a whole month. At such times, I would sit and stare vacantly into the distance with tears trickling down my face. I would stare out of the big glass sliding door at the woods and sky, and when the weather was fine, the tears would flow even more.

Sometimes, the cat would amble across the verandah, behind which the forsythias and komezakura tree glittered in full bloom, and I would look at him, thinking about what strange creatures cats are. For years he had lived with us and all that time, irrespective of whether we get on well or badly, he had never spent a night away from home or gone on a trip. He had just taken it for granted that we would feed him and let him sleep wherever he liked. I felt that he should at least say "Thank you very much for everything". Or perhaps he could comfort me by licking away my tears and saying : "It was very hard for me when your son was little and used to pull me by the tail. But I'm sure that everything will be alright in the end. In fact, it was those difficult times which made a real cat of me. Thank you very much." Or at least he could manage something like : "I'm sure that these stresses and strains are simply a necessary phase for him to grow into a truly splendid man."

However, all the cat did was to open his insolent looking half-closed eyes, flop down on a sunny spot of the floor and devote himself to licking his belly. Suddenly I felt a burst of irritation. "Why is it only you who is never bothered by anything ?" I shouted and gave the cat an unnecessary kick. Nimbly, he jumped on top of a cupboard.

Since then the years have passed and the period of strains and stresses is long since over. The glaring adolescent is now a charming young man. He has also left the nest. The cat however is still with me. Moreover, there has been an addition to the family. I have met a man and we are passionately in love with each other. Outside the green of early summer burns and a cool wind blows in through the open windows. We sit together and gaze out. Can you believe that there is anybody in the world happier than the two of us ?

At such times, the cat quietly walks over and curls up between us. The two of us laugh very gently and stroke him. "What a good little puss !", we say. "What makes cats perfect is the fact that they never say anything. You make our happiness perfect. What a good little puss !" We laugh gently.

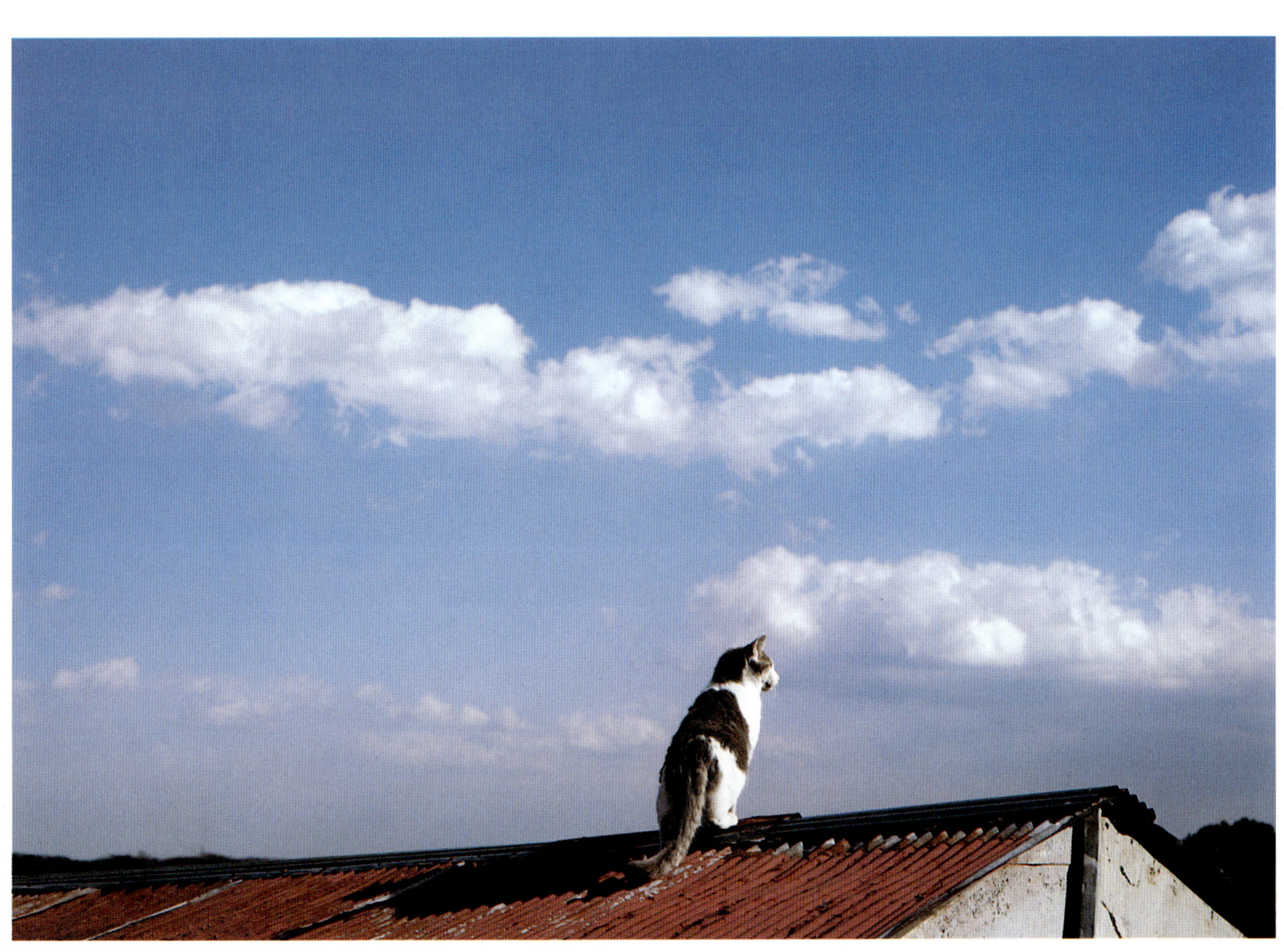

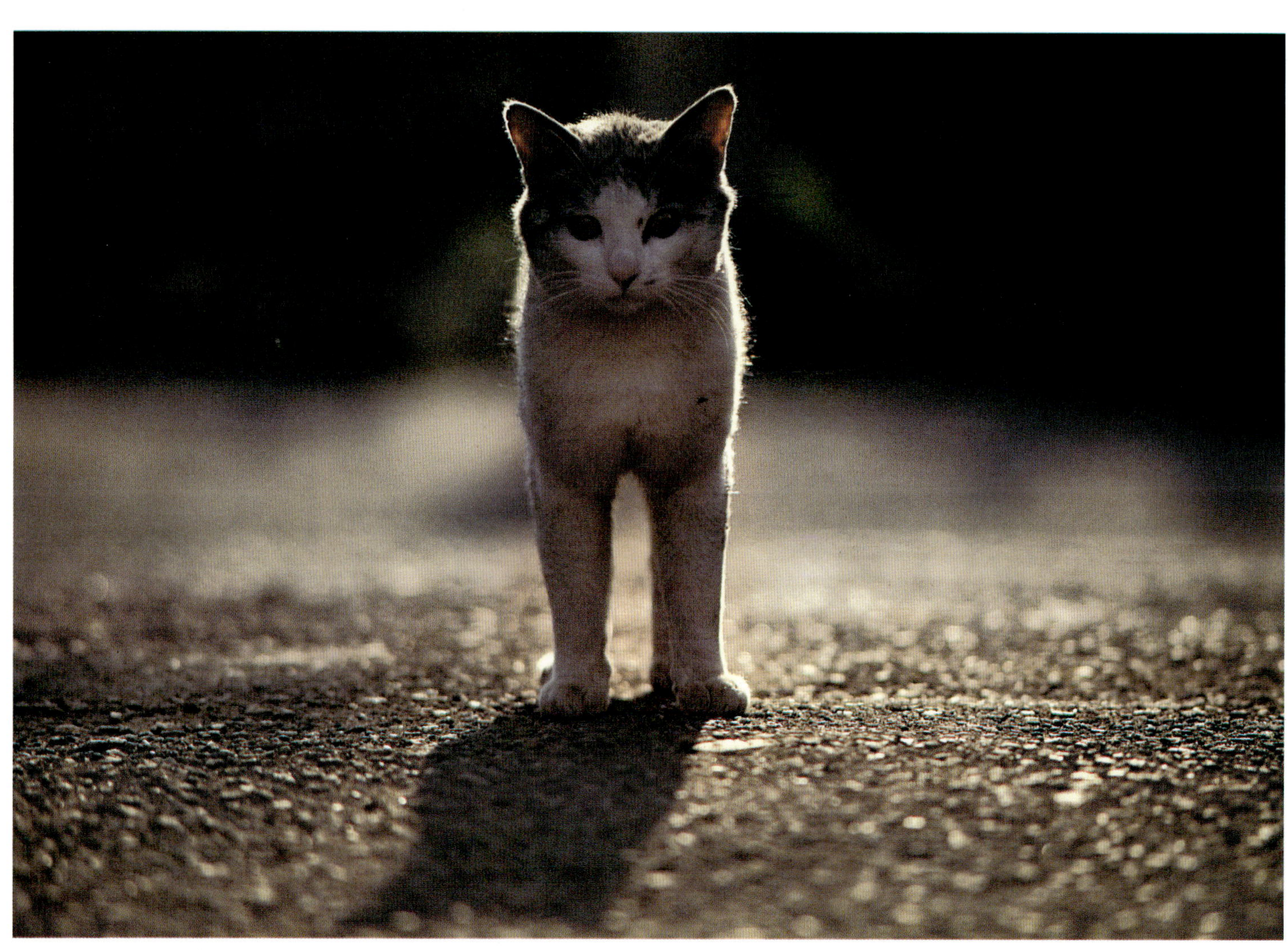

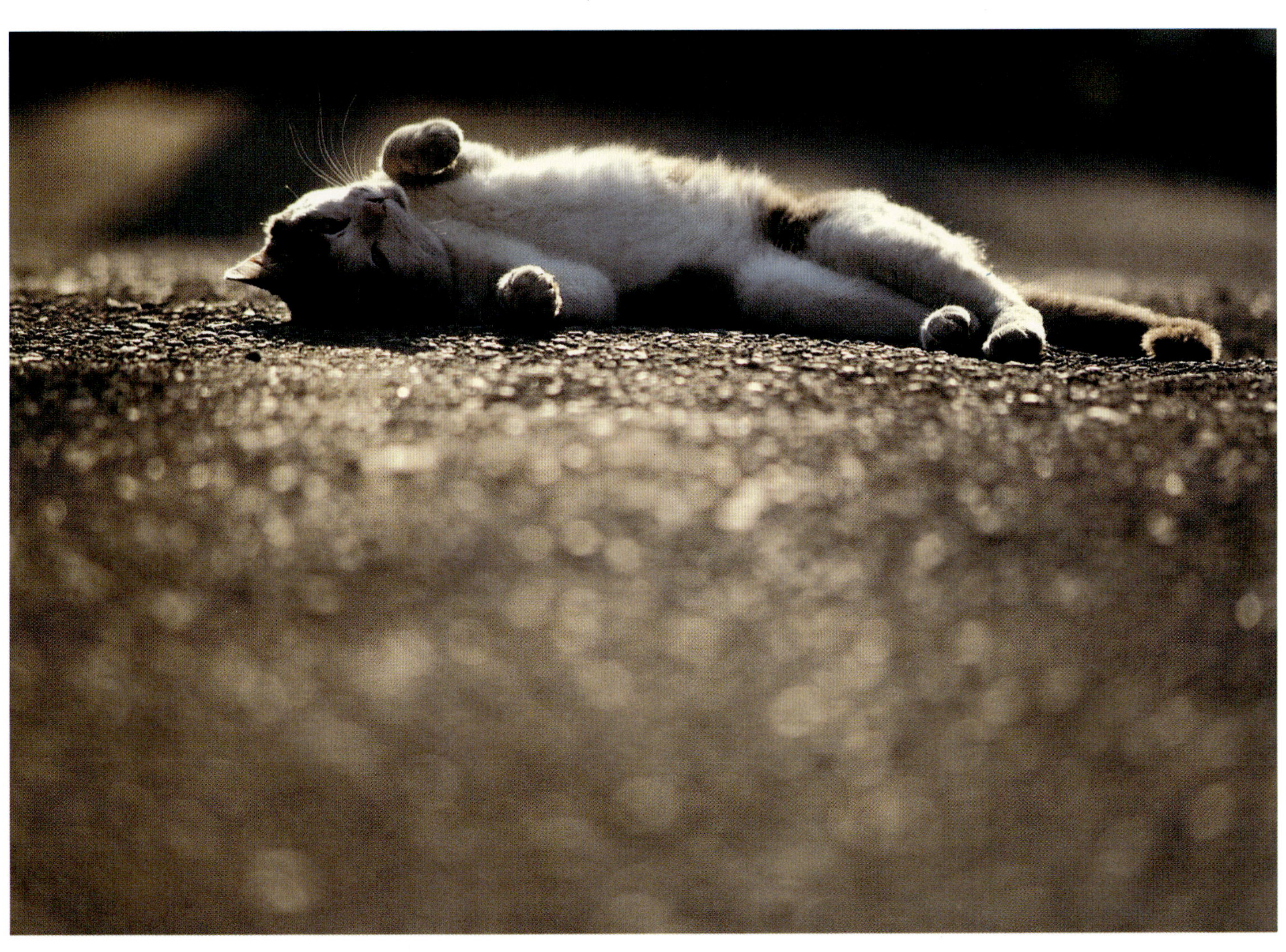

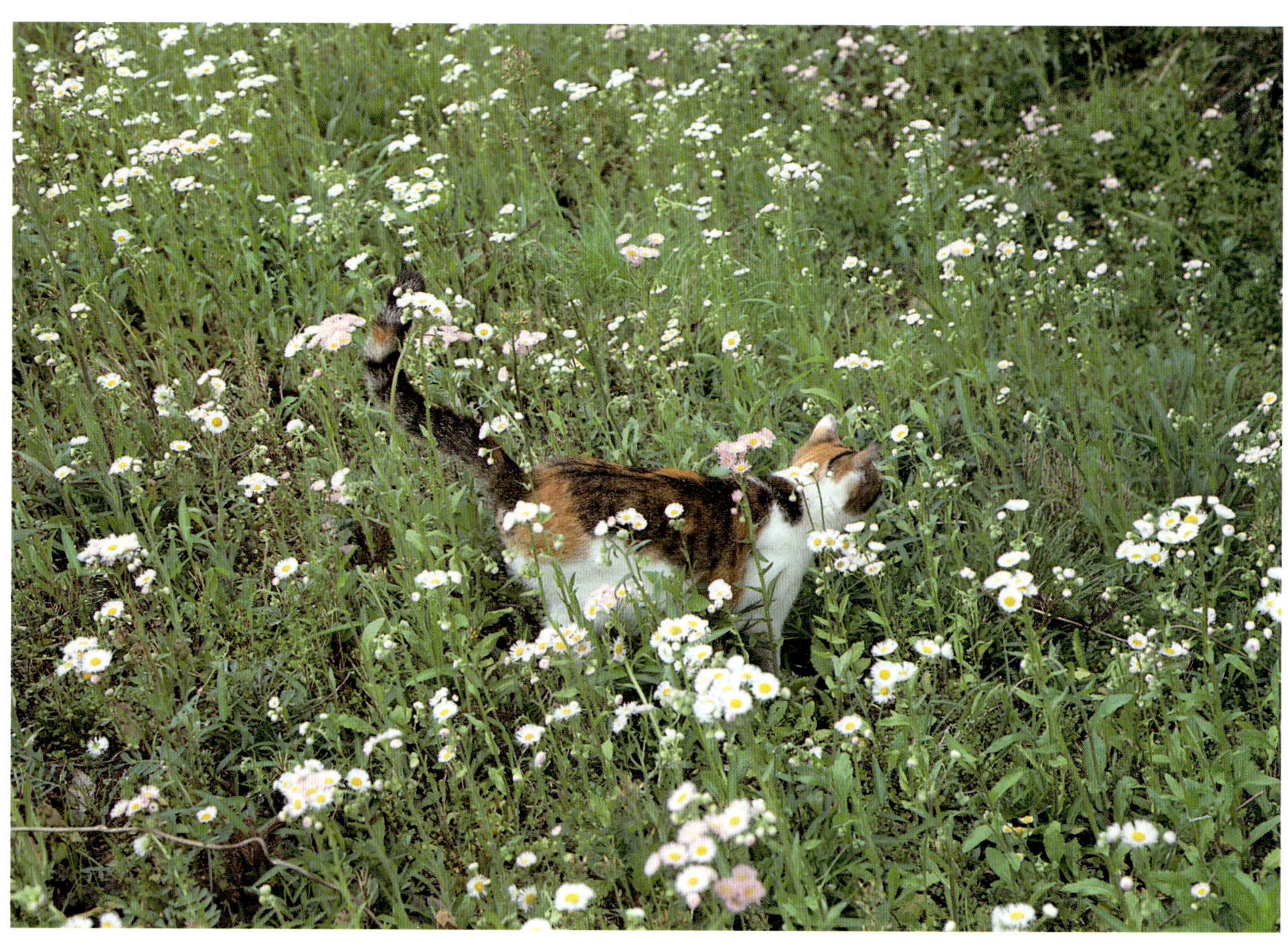

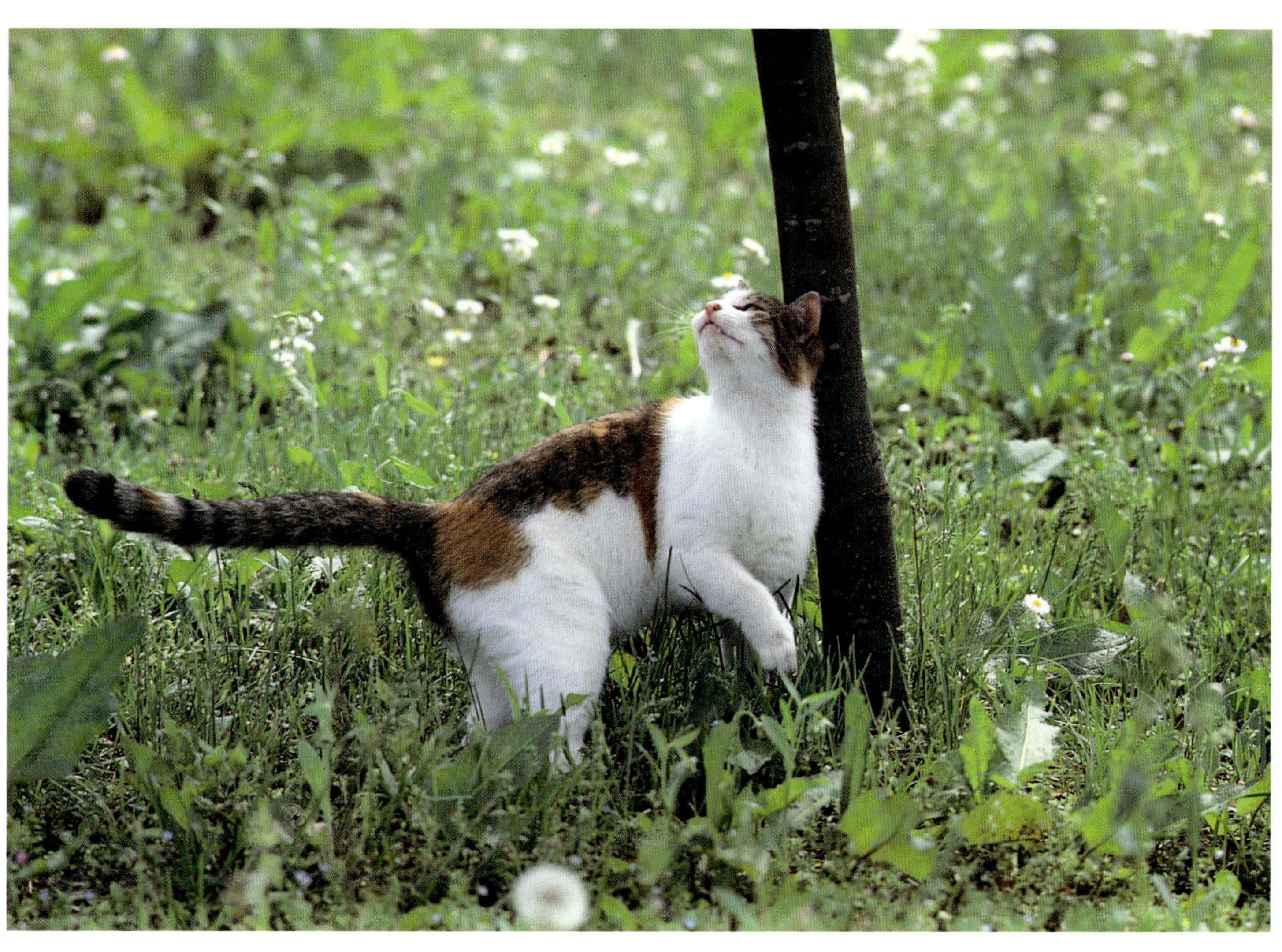

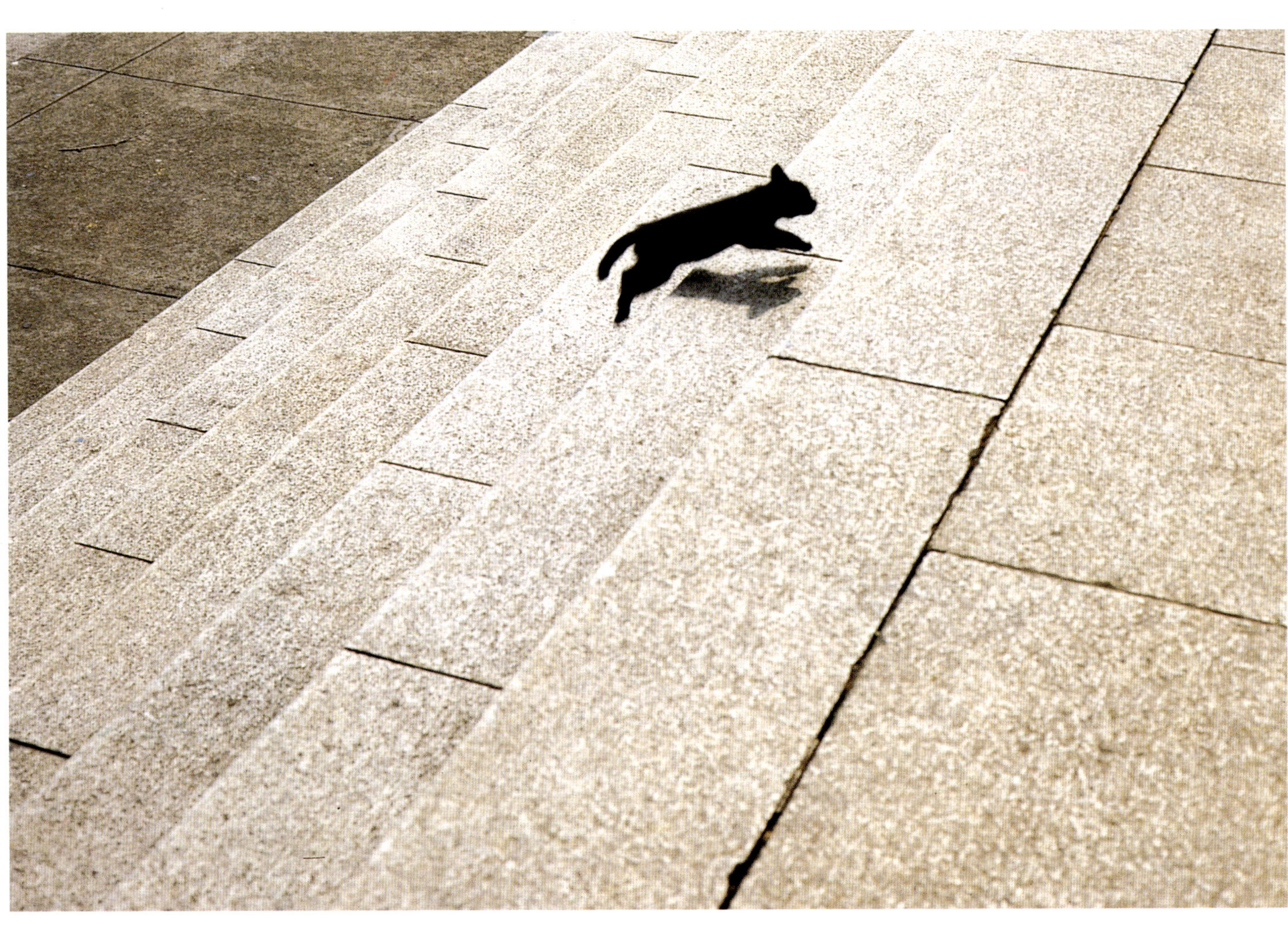

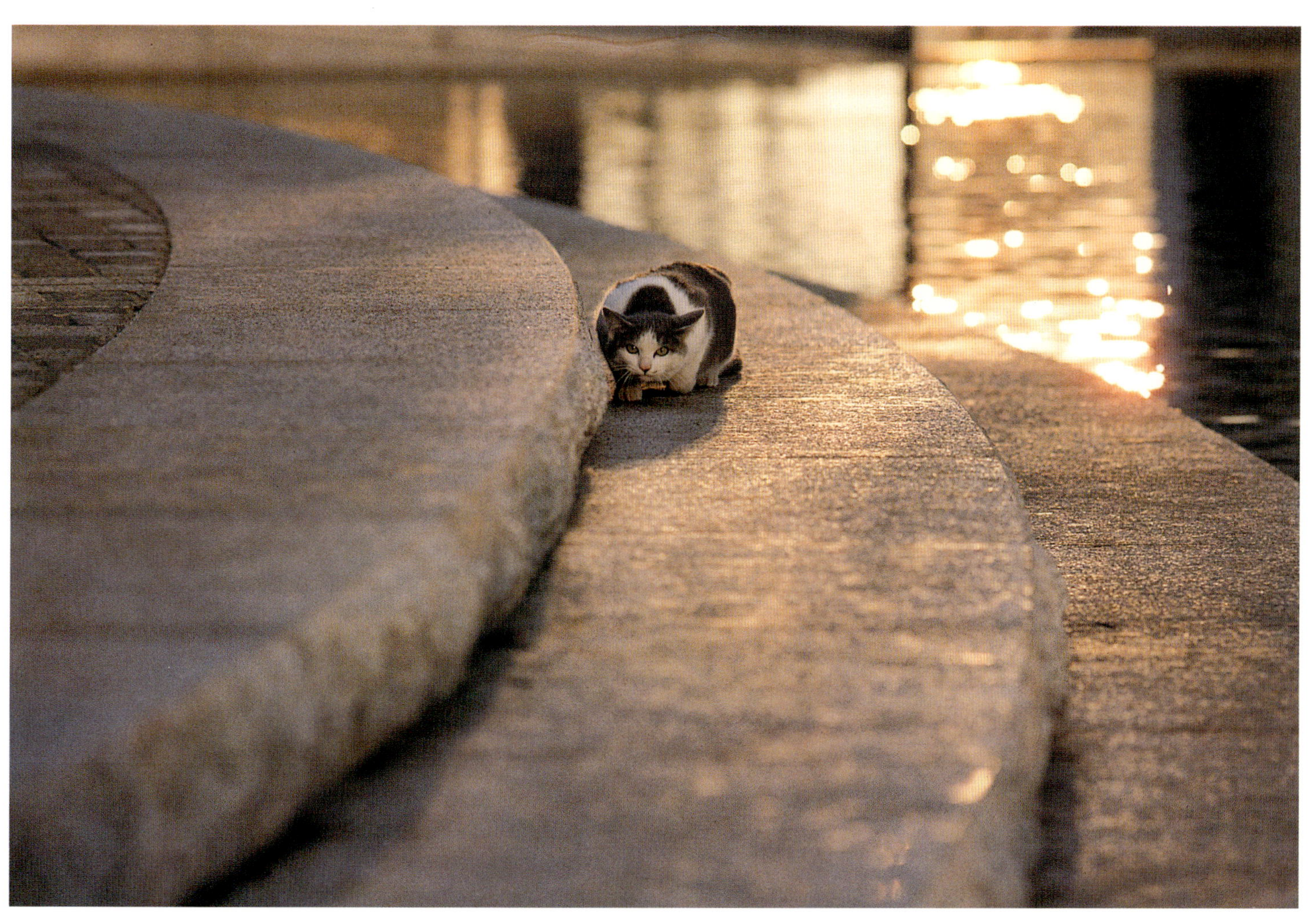

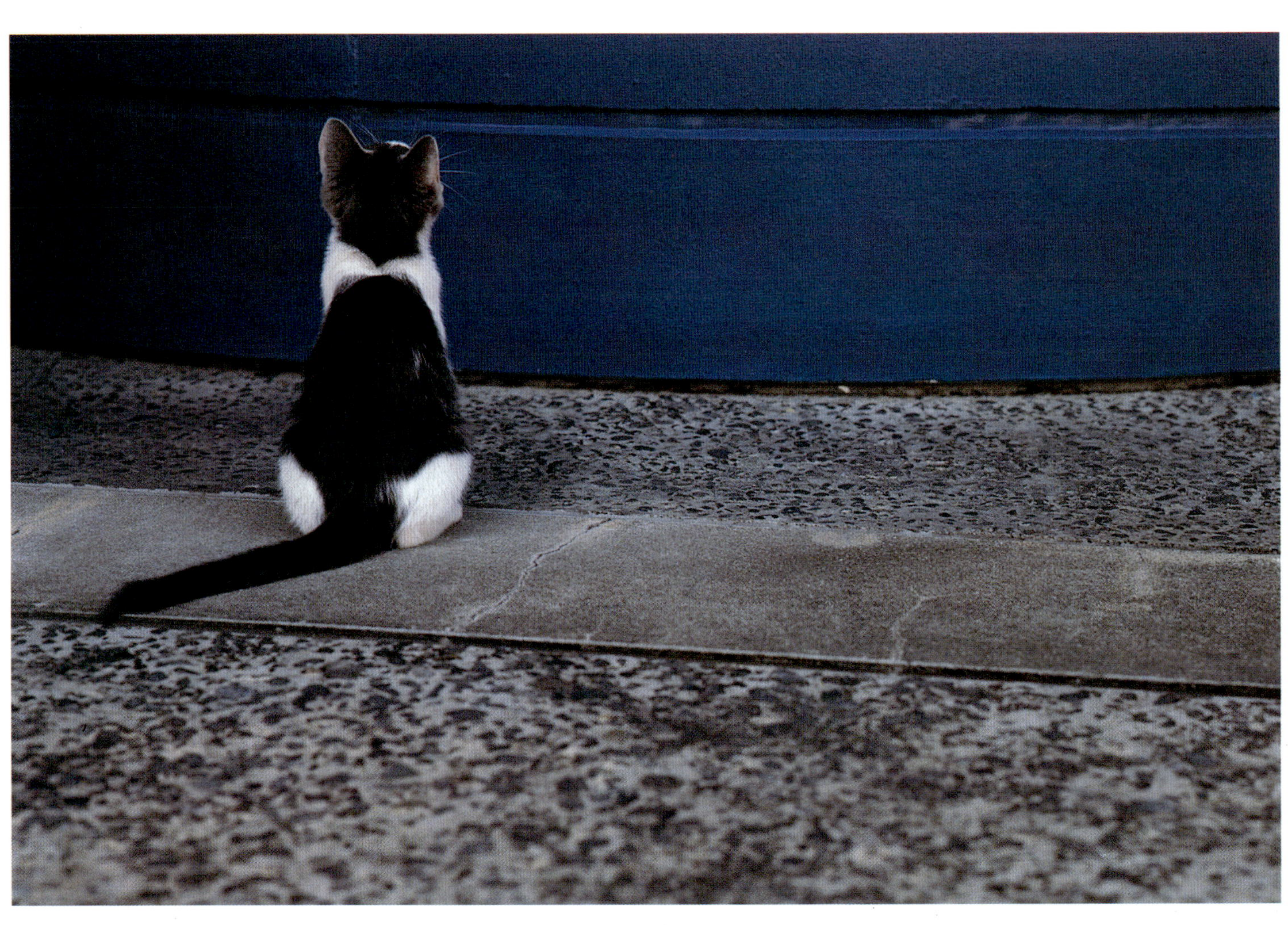

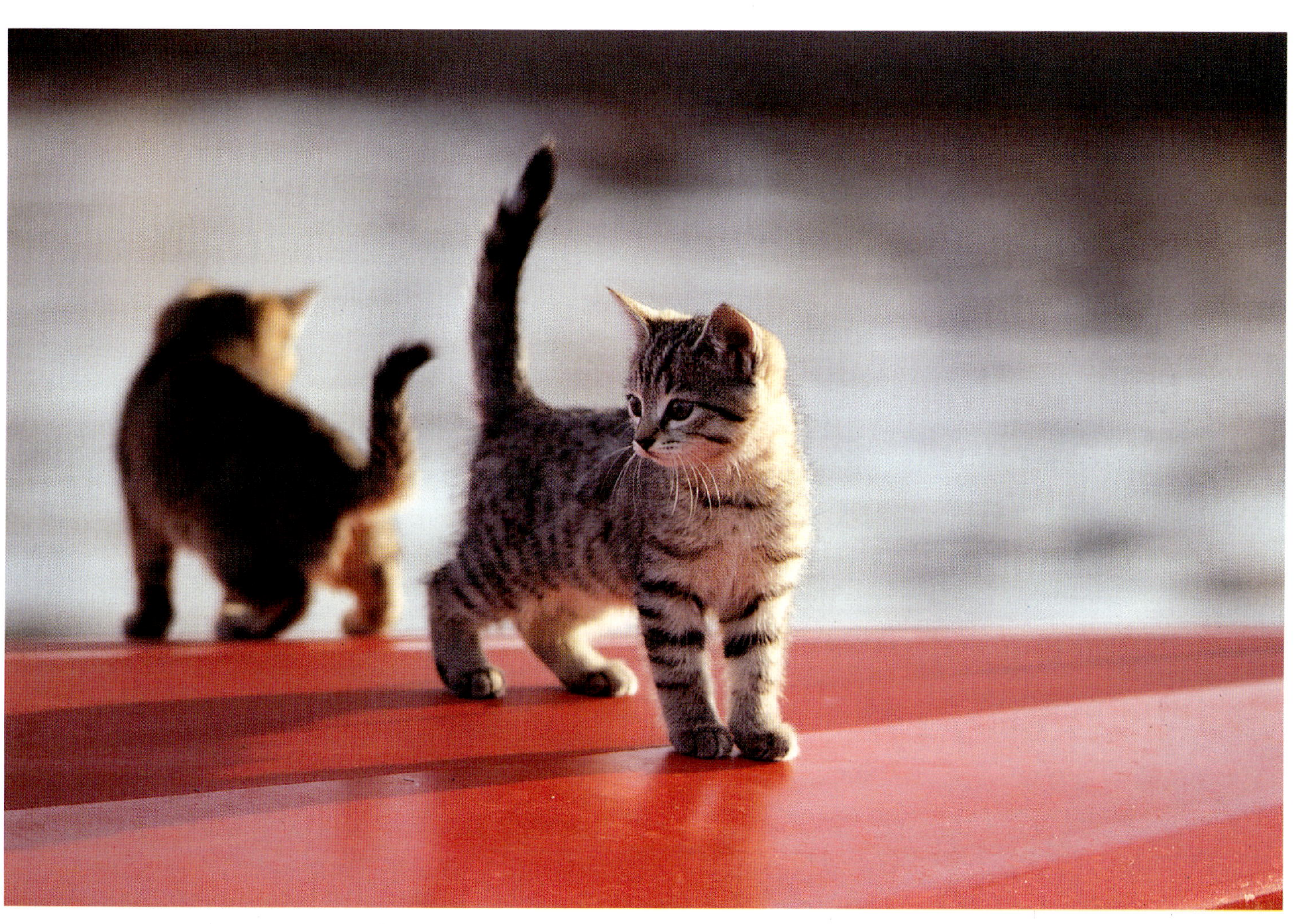

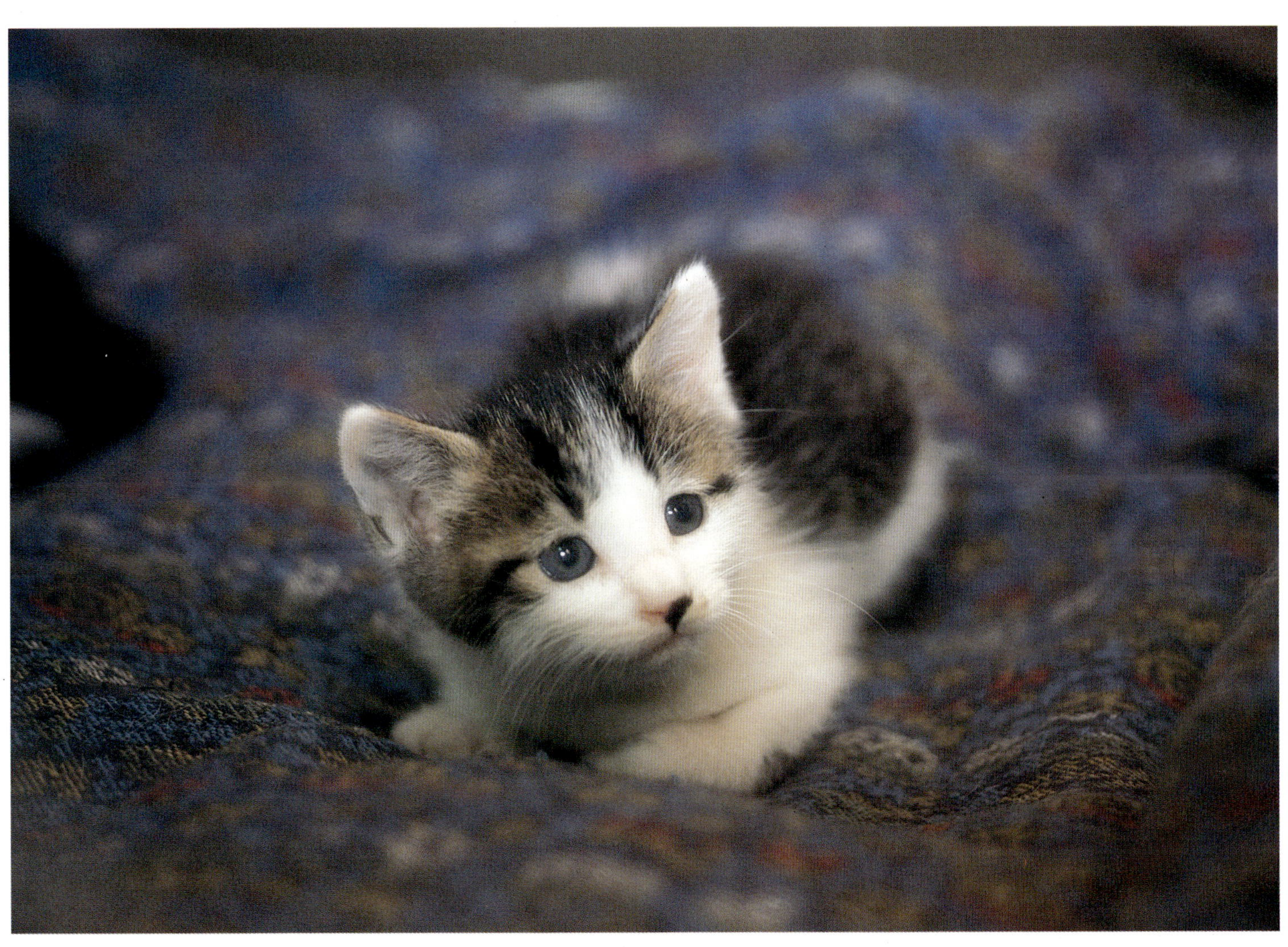

猫のいる町

川本三郎
文芸評論家

水天宮を中心とした日本橋人形町界隈は東京の町のなかでもとりわけ好きなところで週に一，二度は足を運ぶ。戦災にあわなかったために古い家並がかろうじて残っている。江戸時代からの町だから老舗がたくさんあって落着いている。

最近，この町は非常に猫が多いことに気づいた。

まず飼猫が多い。商店街のあちこちで猫を飼っている。そば屋には黒と白の大きな猫がいる。もうそうとうな年らしくよく店先で眠っている。その向かいの八百屋には茶色のトラ猫がいる。うなぎ屋には仔猫がいる。とんかつ屋には三毛猫がいる。ビルのあいだにはさまれた木造の二軒家はお婆さんのひとり暮しと見受けられるがここには猫が５，６匹はいる。

野良猫も多い。車の量が減ってくる夜になるとあちこちから猫があらわれる。集会をはじめる。角ごとに猫の姿があるといっても大仰ではない。塀の上にいる。ビルとビルの間の狭い隙間にいる。猫だらけである。

人形町にはなぜこんなに猫が多いのか。

古くからある町で町全体にゆとりがあるというのがひとつの理由だろう。路地と神社が多く猫にとっては安全だということも考えられる。昔は花街だったところだから，いまでも料理家が多く野良猫が住みやすいということもあるだろう。マンションより個人の家のほうが多いために「猫を飼ってはいけない」という規制もないのだろう。

猫が多いことに気づいてから人形町がますます好きになった。あるとき人形町に一泊し早朝の町を散歩する機会があった。と，お婆さんが町かどごとでしゃがんで何かしているのに出会った。何をしているのか不思議に思って見ていると彼女は野良猫にエサをやっていた。手かごにエサをいっぱい入れて町じゅうを回っている。彼女の姿を見るとあちこちの路地裏から猫があらわれる。

私はいよいよこの町が好きになってしまった。

A Neighbourhood Full of Cats

Saburo Kawamoto
Literary Critic

Out of Tokyo's many neighbourhoods, one of my favourites is Ningyocho in Nihonbashi, which is centred around the old Suitengu Shinto shrine. In fact I visit this area as often as once or twice a week. Because it largely escaped damage in the War, there still remain a few streets of traditional houses. This part of Tokyo has existed since the Edo Period and so many old businesses survive, giving the neighbourhood a calm and settled atmosphere.

Recently, I have become aware of the fact that an extraordinarily large number of cats live in this area.

First of all, there are many pet cats here. In the shopping street, in particular, you can find pet cats all over the place. A big black and white cat lives at the noodle restaurant; apparently it is already pretty old and it spends much of its time sleeping in front of the shop. A brown tabby lives at the greengrocer's opposite. There is a kitten at the broiled eel restaurant, and a tortoiseshell at the pork cutlet restaurant. In a little wooden two-storey house, squeezed between two large modern buildings, an old lady seems to be living alone with five or six cats.

There are also a lot of alley cats here. Especially at night, when the number of cars drops, alley cats begin to appear from all over the place. It is time for the nightly gathering to convene, and it is no exaggeration to say that cats appear at every single corner, on the tops of walls, in the narrow cracks between buildings. The whole area is covered with cats.

Why are cats so common in Ningyocho?

Perhaps one reason is that whole area has had a relaxed and leisurely atmosphere since the old days. Again, the profusion of alleys and shrines probably makes it an especially safe place for cats. Another reason is that this area was in the old days a geisha district and so even today there are many restaurants here, which makes life a little easier for alley cats. Moreover, because there are far more ordinary houses than big apartment blocks, there are no regulations to prevent people from keeping cats.

Since I became conscious of how many cats live in Ningyocho I have come to like the area even more than before. The other day I had occasion to spend the night in Ningyocho and to walk through the neighbourhood early in the morning. As I did so, I came across an old lady bending over at the corner of the street and doing something. I wondered what on earth she was up to, but as I watched I realised that she was giving food to the alley cats. Clutching a basket full of food, she was walking around the whole area. When the alley cats saw her coming, they came out of each little alley or lane.

When I saw that, I fell even more deeply in love with this neighbourhood.

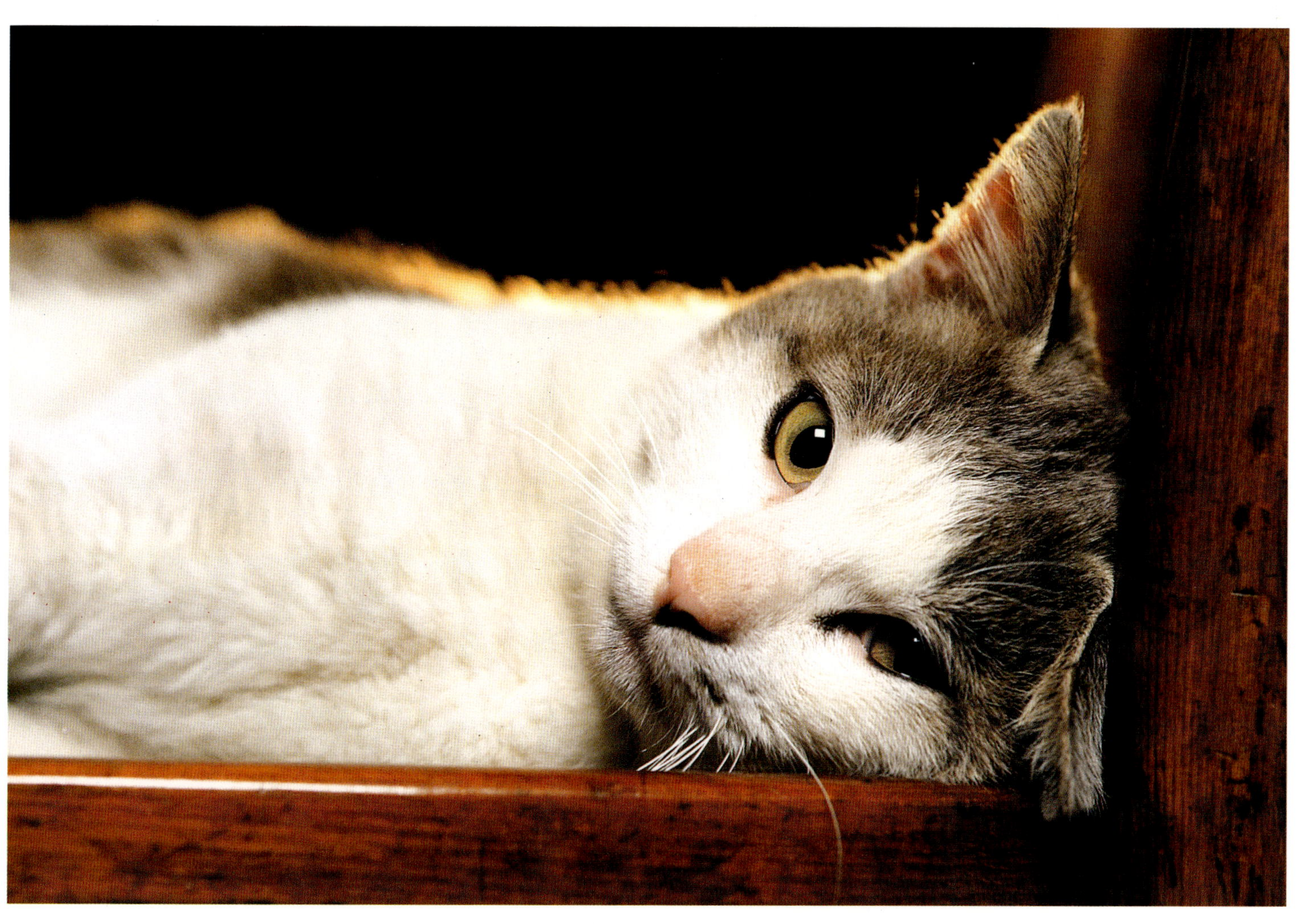

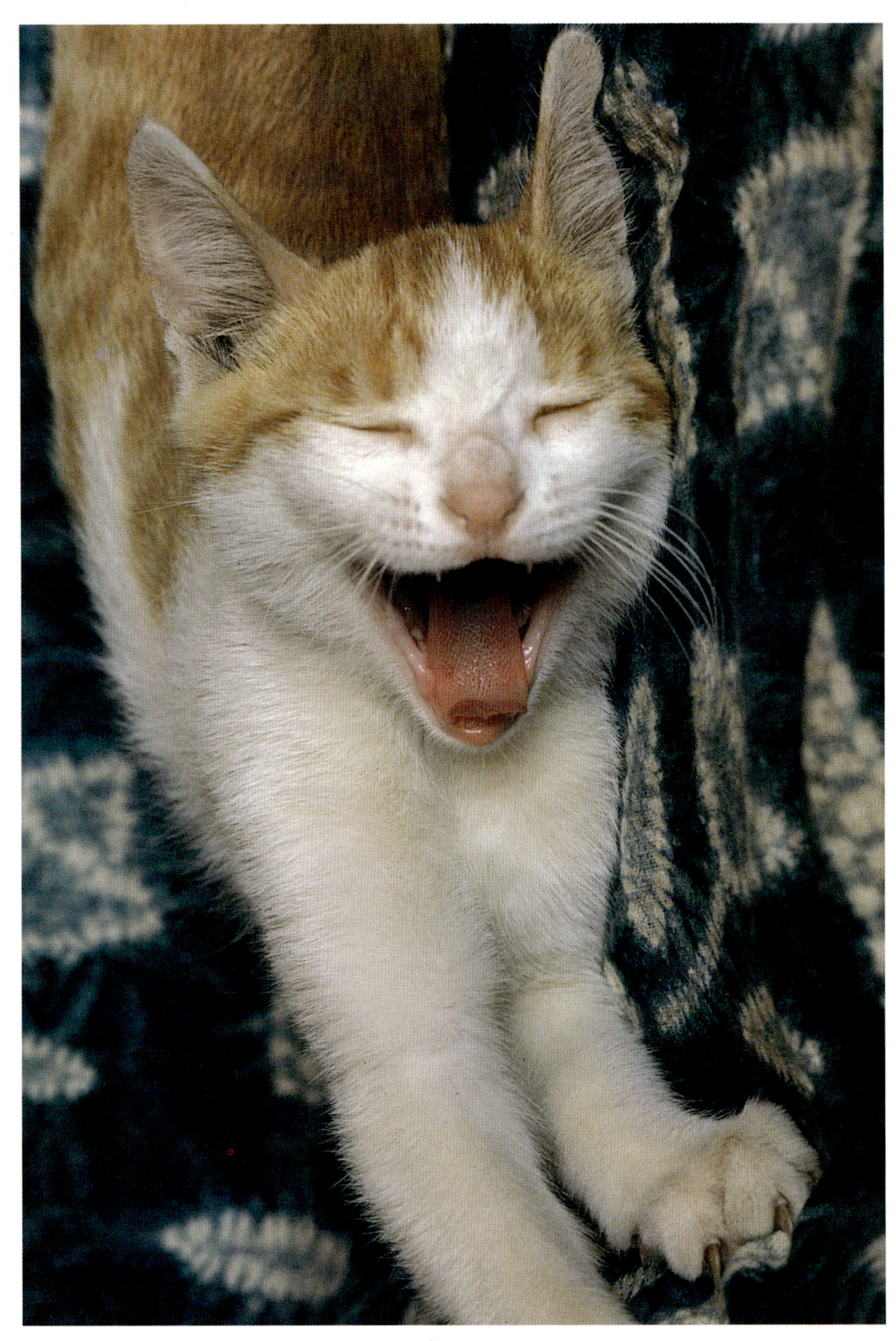

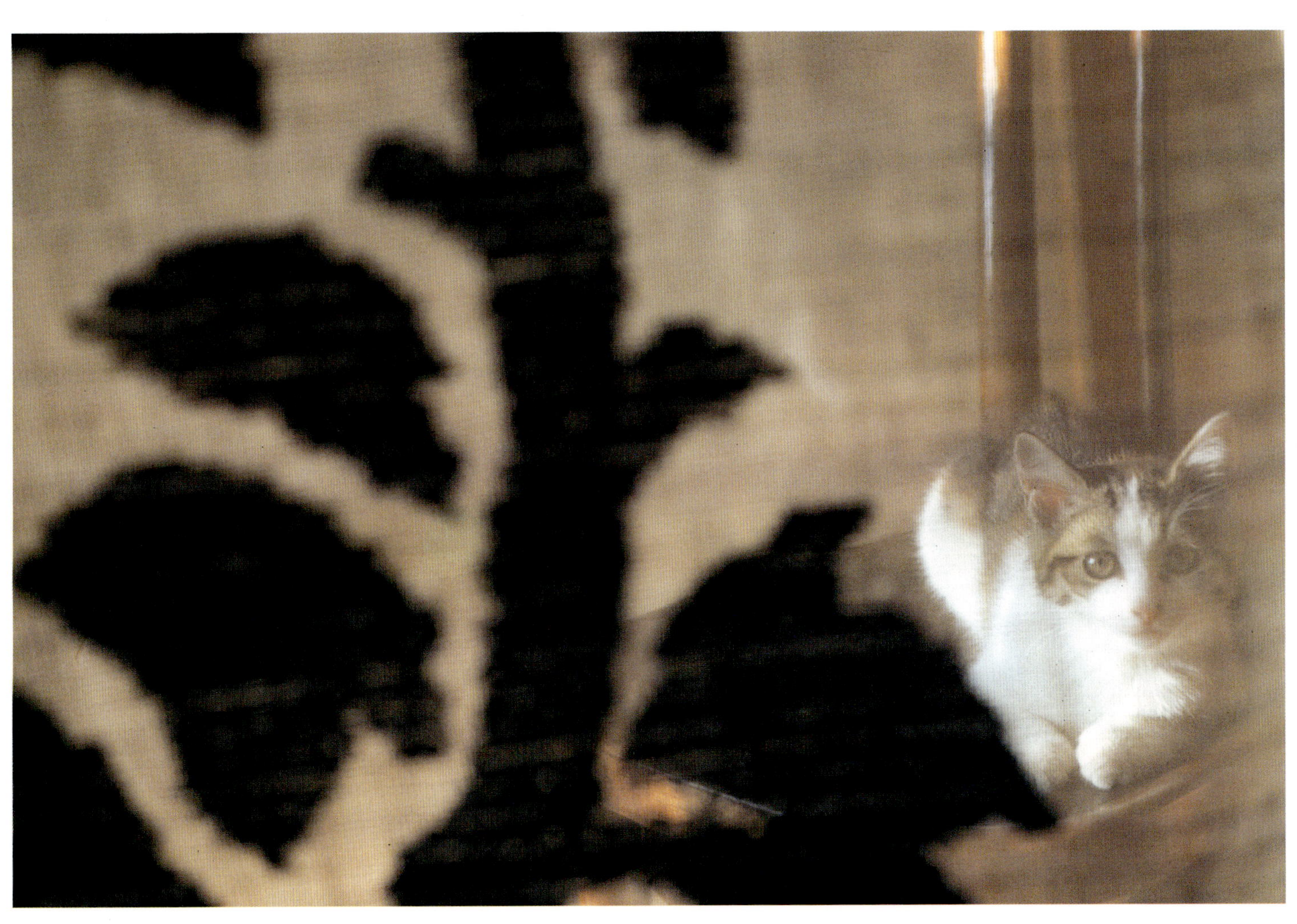

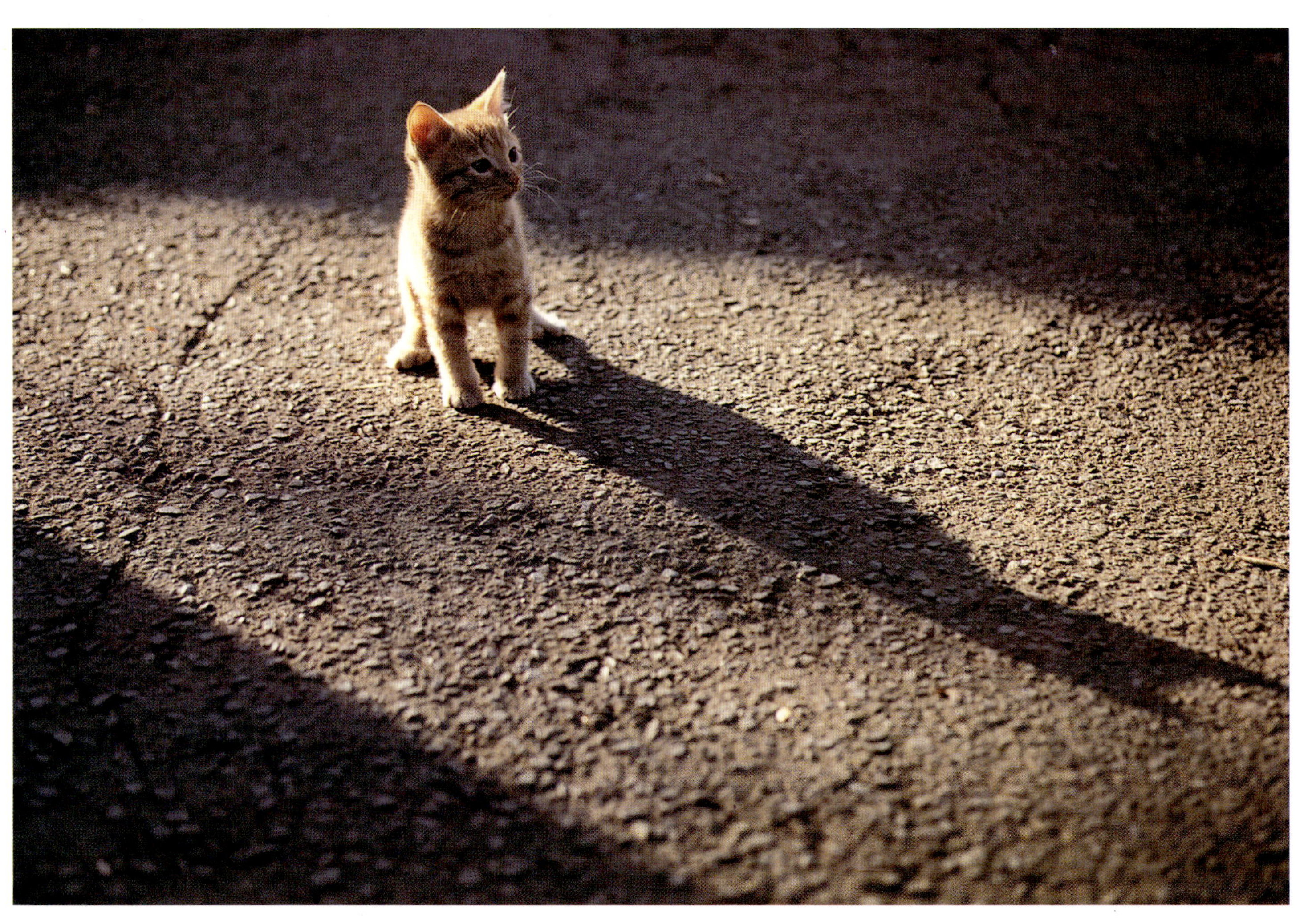

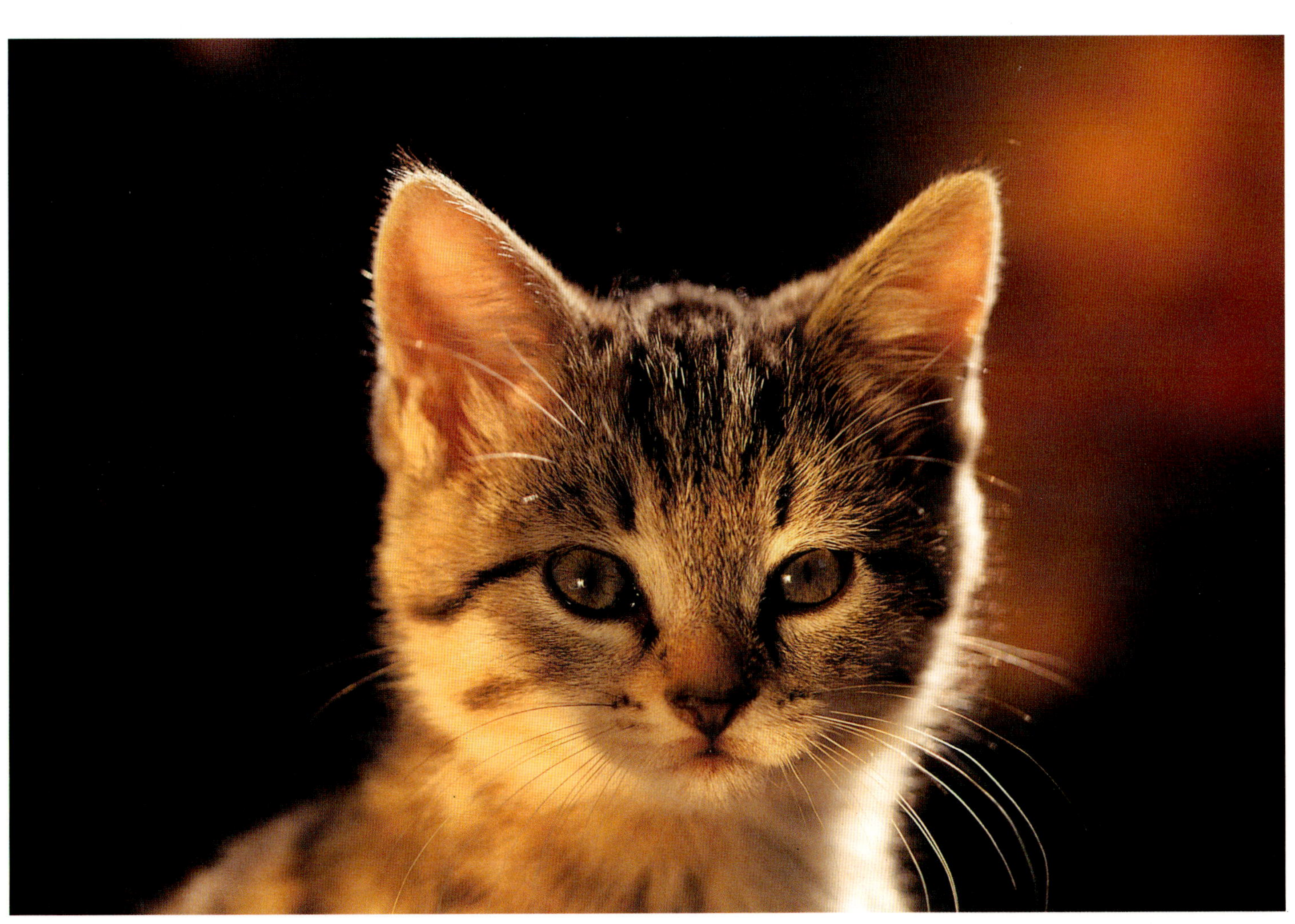

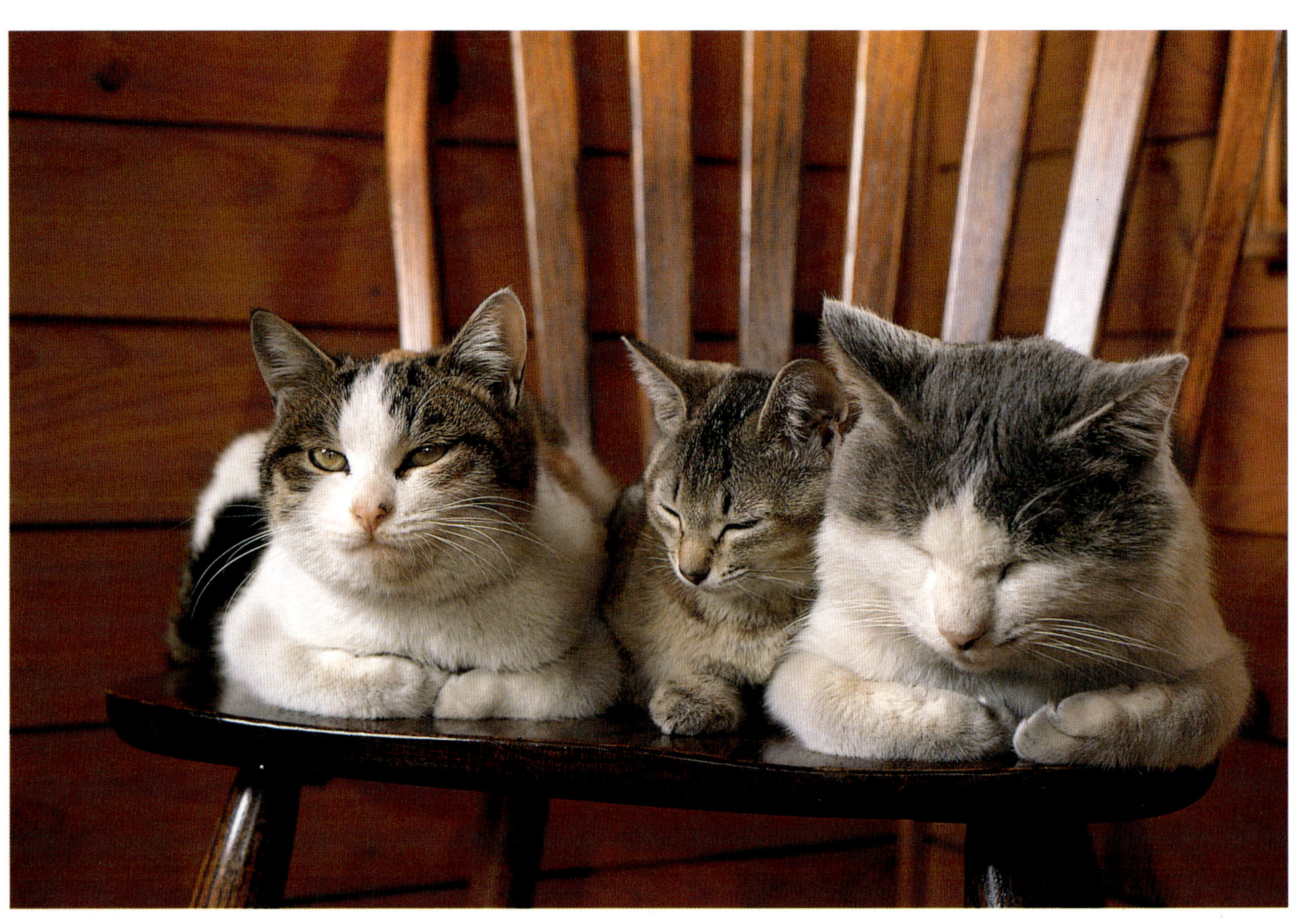

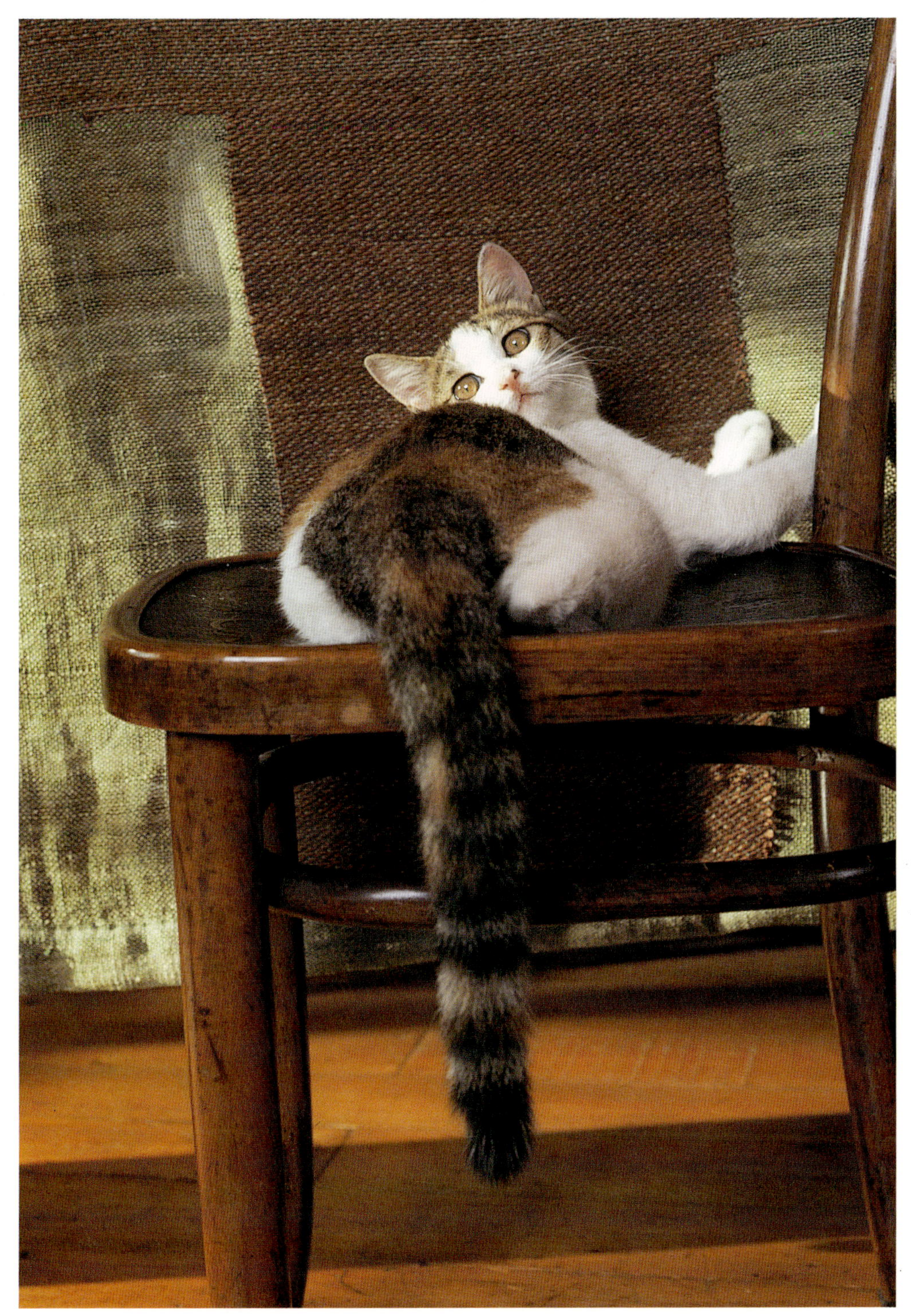

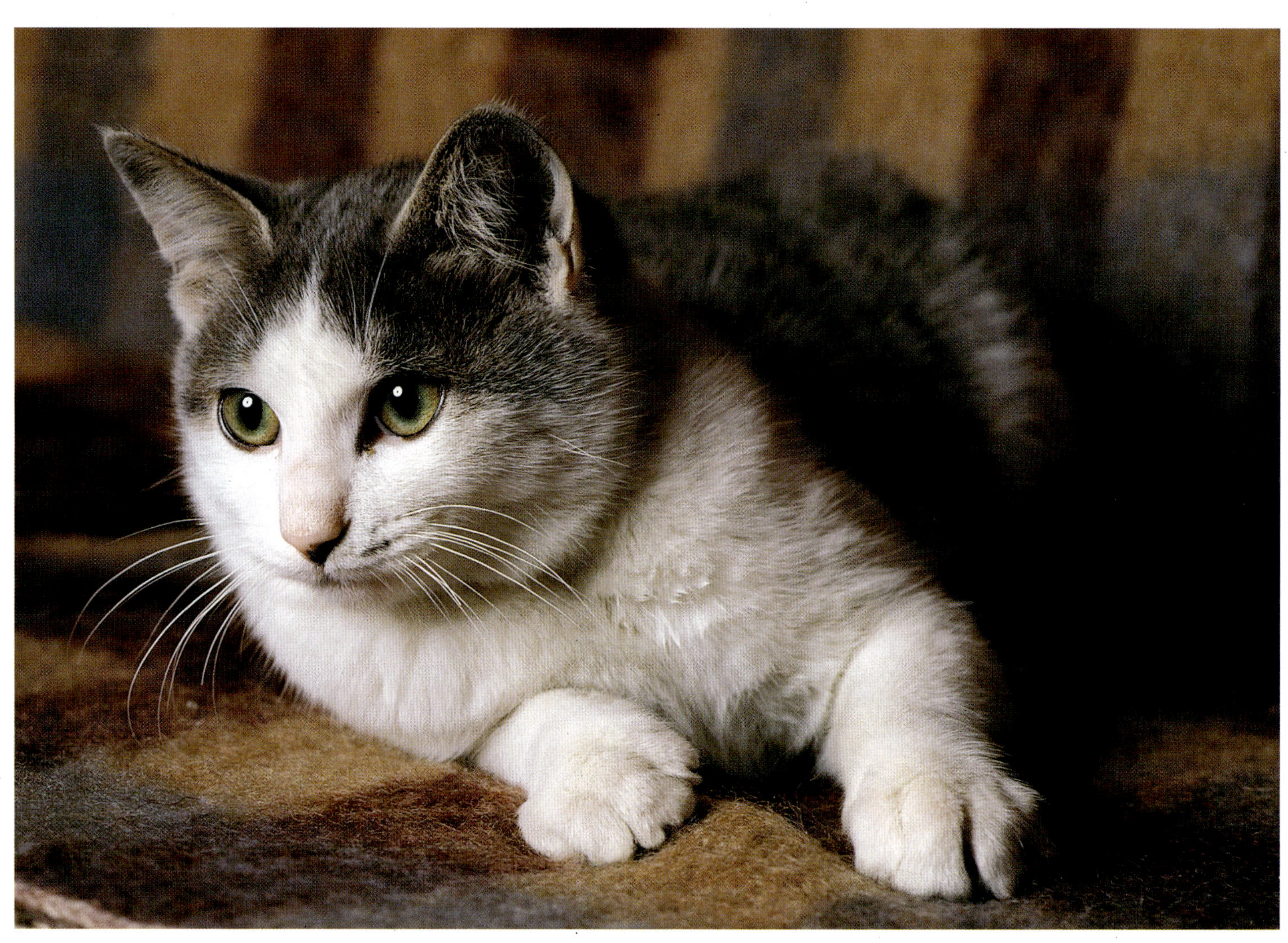

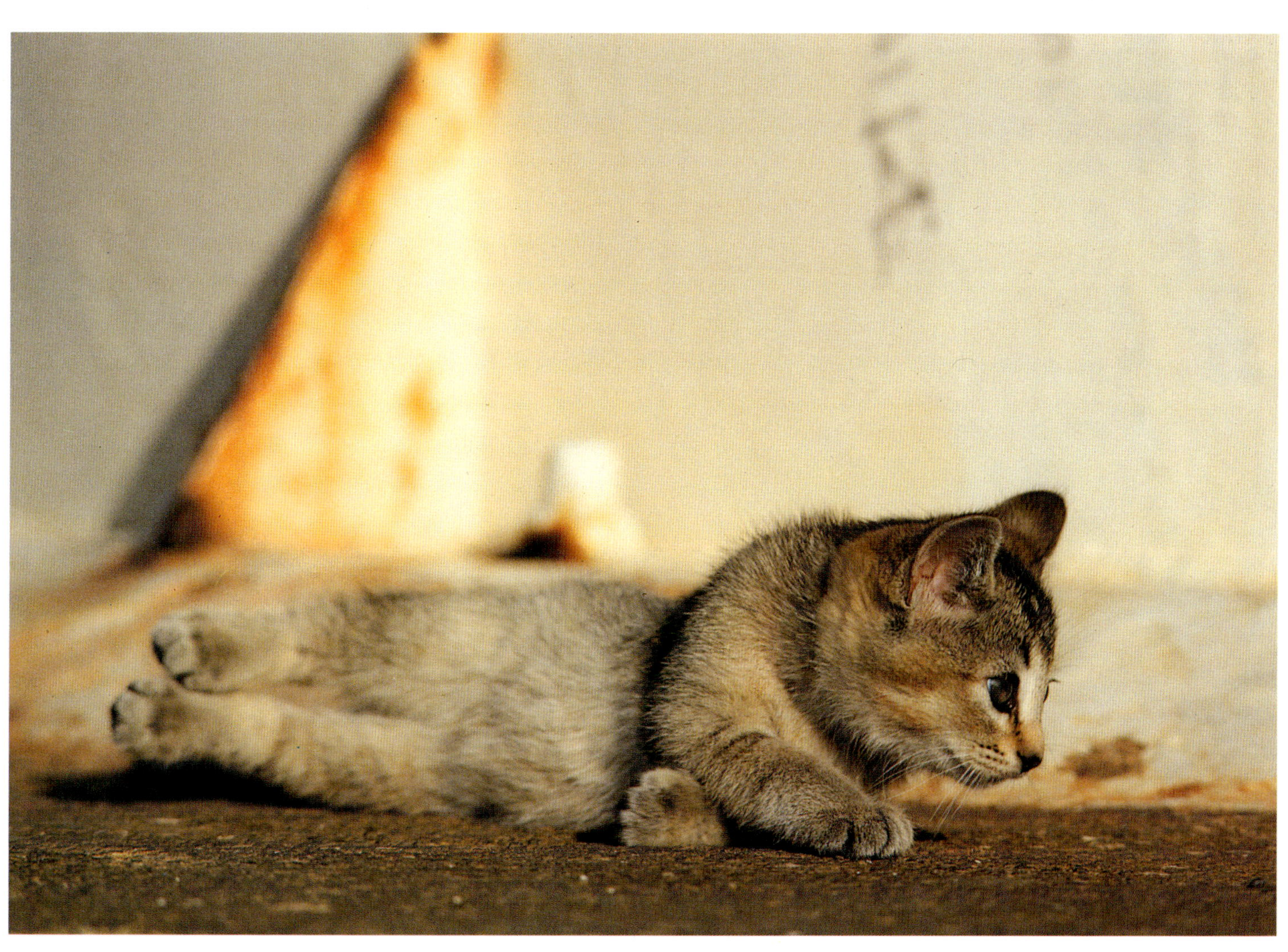

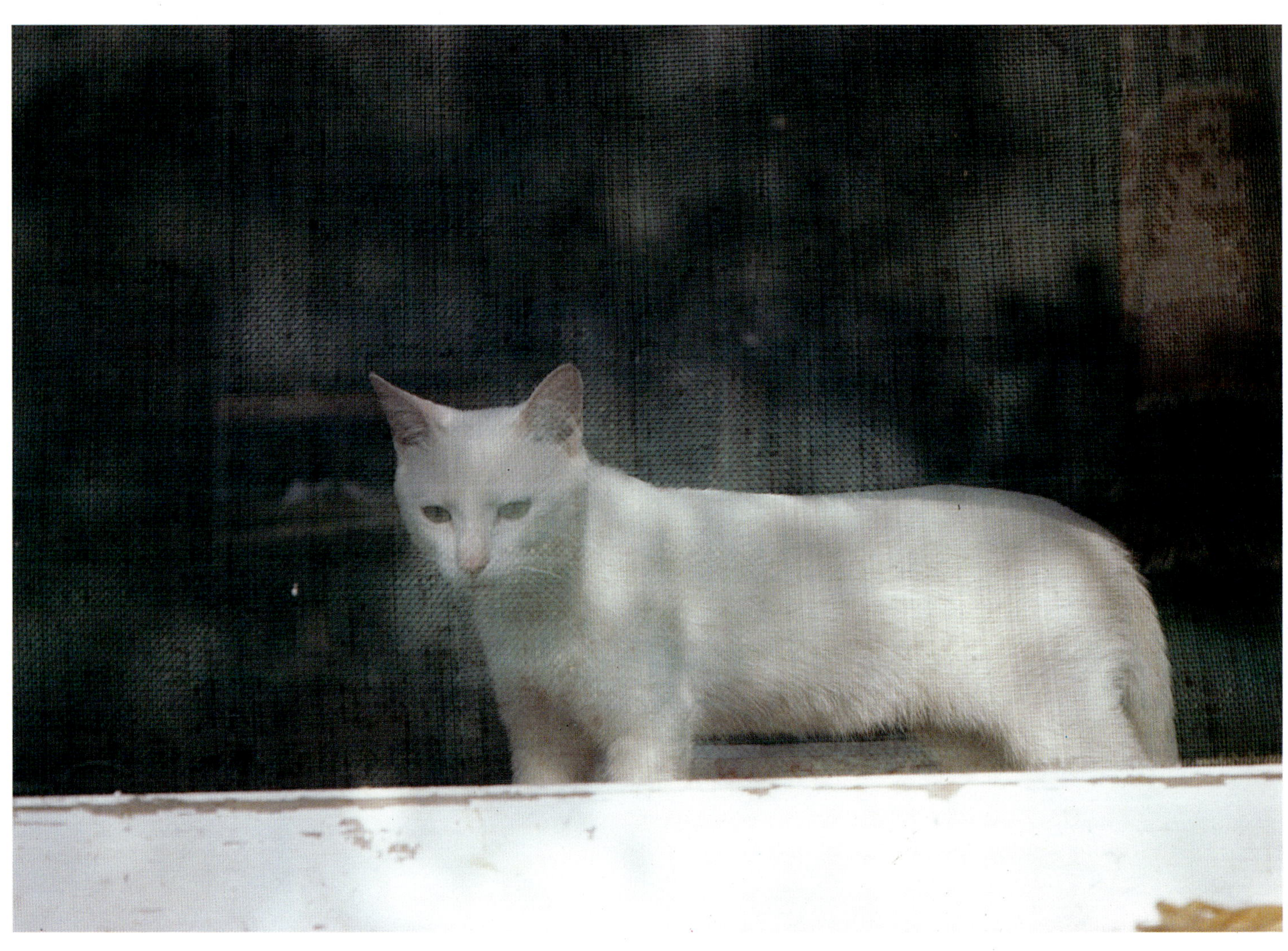

猫又

中沢けい
作家

猫が人をおそうという話は聞いたことがない。いたって臆病であるか，慎重であるか，あるいは猛獣の末裔らしく無益な争いは好まずと冷静であるか，その態度は猫によりけりだが，いずれにしても人と猫は微妙に生活の領分をわけ合いながら静かに暮している。こうした事実から考えると，化け猫の話が在るのはまことに不思議だが，しかし，古くから言われ続けてきたことでもある。

兼好法師の徒然草に猫又の事が見える。山にあって人を喰うと言う人もいれば，年功をへた猫のなり果てたものと言う人もいるとある。猫の，見方によっては人を嫌うような，また人に対してはあまりにも冷淡な様子がこのようなものを生み出したのであろうか。確かに争うことはない。それと等しく温順とは感じられない。あの猫の瞳が世の人の姿をうつしながら年月を積み重ねた果てに，激しい嫌悪の衝動を宿しはしないかという想像が生まれる道理は，そこはかとなく感じることができる。特に世俗の利益を追うことに忙しく，自己の得失を推るに息をつく閑もないといった世相にあっては，なおさら，猫の持つ上品さが不気味に覚えられたことであろう。兼好法師の生きた中世中期はどうやら，そのような世相の時代であった様子だ。

かえりみるに，現今はいかがであろうか。猫を猫又に変化させるほど世の中の欲望は深いのであろうか。猫の身ではなく，人の身で東京の街に佇んでいると，利益を追うことにも忙しく，得失の勘定もしのぎを削りはしているが，欲望が深いというには人々の表情に精気がなさすぎるところが目に付くのだった。そして，欲望を持つには疲れ過ぎていると思わせる。これでは，自分の欲望の満たし方の程というものをわきまえた猫の暮しは，人からうらまれるかもしれない。人又。まさかとは思うが，猫たちがそのような話を仲間から仲間へと伝えていはしないだろうか。

Nekomata

Kei Nakazawa
Author

I have never heard of a cat attacking a human beng. This may be due to cowardice or to caution, or it may be that cats, as the final result of a long process of evolution from wild beasts, have become too sophisticated to engage in such futile battles. The explanation probably varies from cat to cat, but whichever is right, it remains a fact that cats and human beings live together peacefully by carefully separating their respective domains. When we think of this fact, however, it seems very odd that there are so many stories in Japan about 'bakeneko', cats who change into monsters and attack people. Such stories are very old.

We can read about the Nekomata, a monstrous cat, in the 14th-century Kenko Hoshi's 'Essays in Idleness' ('Tsurezuregusa') : "Some people say that Nekomata is found in the mountains and eats people ; others say that ordinary cats with age and experience become such monsters." Perhaps this kind of story arose because cats can look as though they really dislike people, or because of the extremely cool attitude which they adopt towards human beings. Certainly cats do not fight with human beings, yet they by no means give the impression of a gentle docility. The idea that years and years of watching coldly the activities of people may issue in some extremely vicious reaction has a kind of logic to it. Particularly in a society where people busily pursue worldly success and continually calculate their own personal profit or loss without a moment's leisure, then that special kind of elegance and poise which a cat possesses can come to seem weird or threatening. The medieval world in which Kenko Hoshi lived does indeed seem to have been just such a time.

How about today ? Is our world greedy enough to transform cats into Nekomata, monster cats ? Looking around the streets of Tokyo, not as a cat, but as a human being, there can be no doubt that people are busily pursuing worldy success and frantically calculating profit and loss. Yet one cannot help noticing that their expressions are too lifeless to be described as truly greedy. Rather they look as though they have been tired out by their own greed. In fact, in this state of affairs, it may be that people will come to resent the way in which cats live, their knowledge of just what is required to achieve satisfaction. Hitomata, monstrous people ! I hope not, but ir may be that even now the cats ate telling one another such stories.

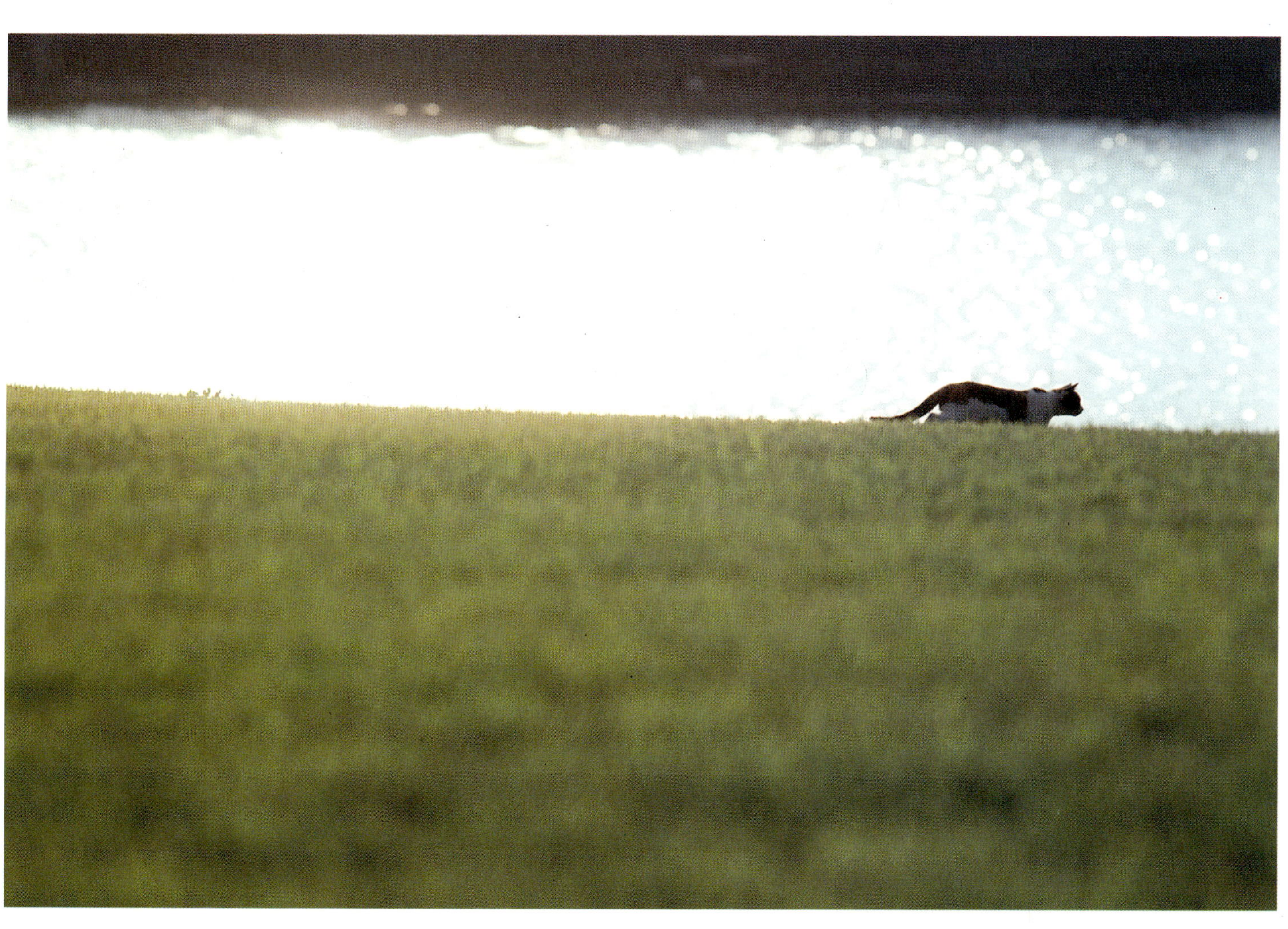

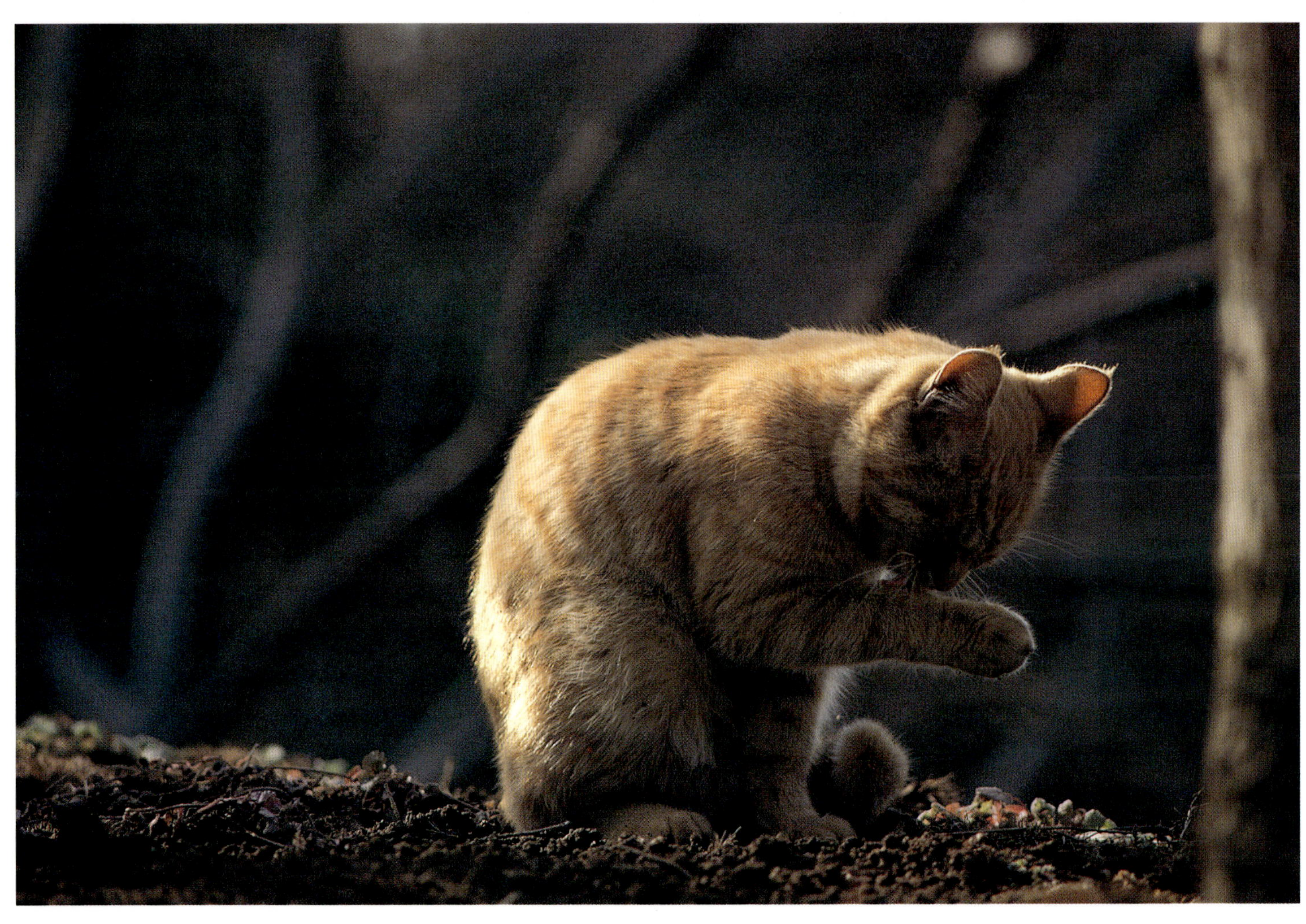

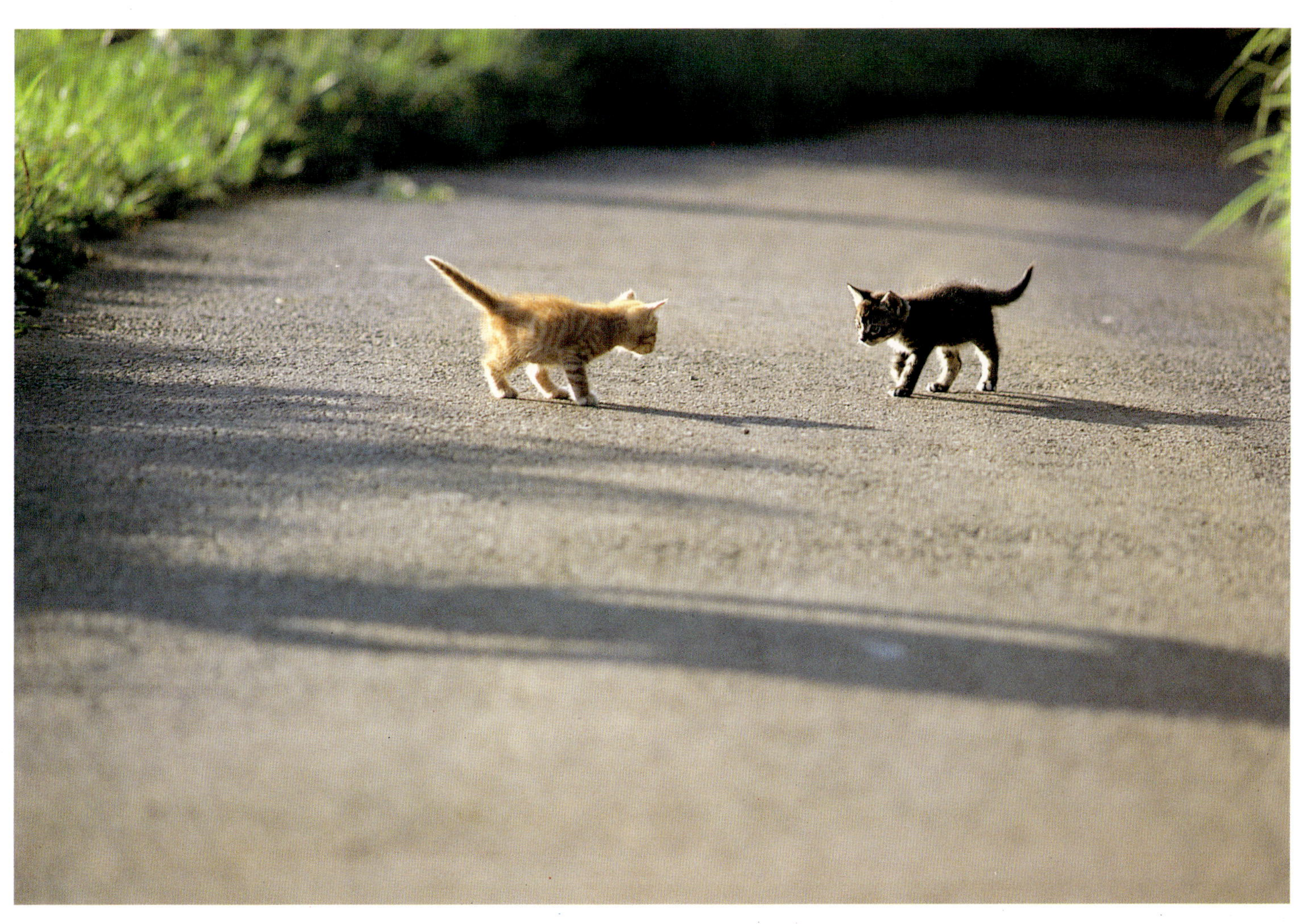

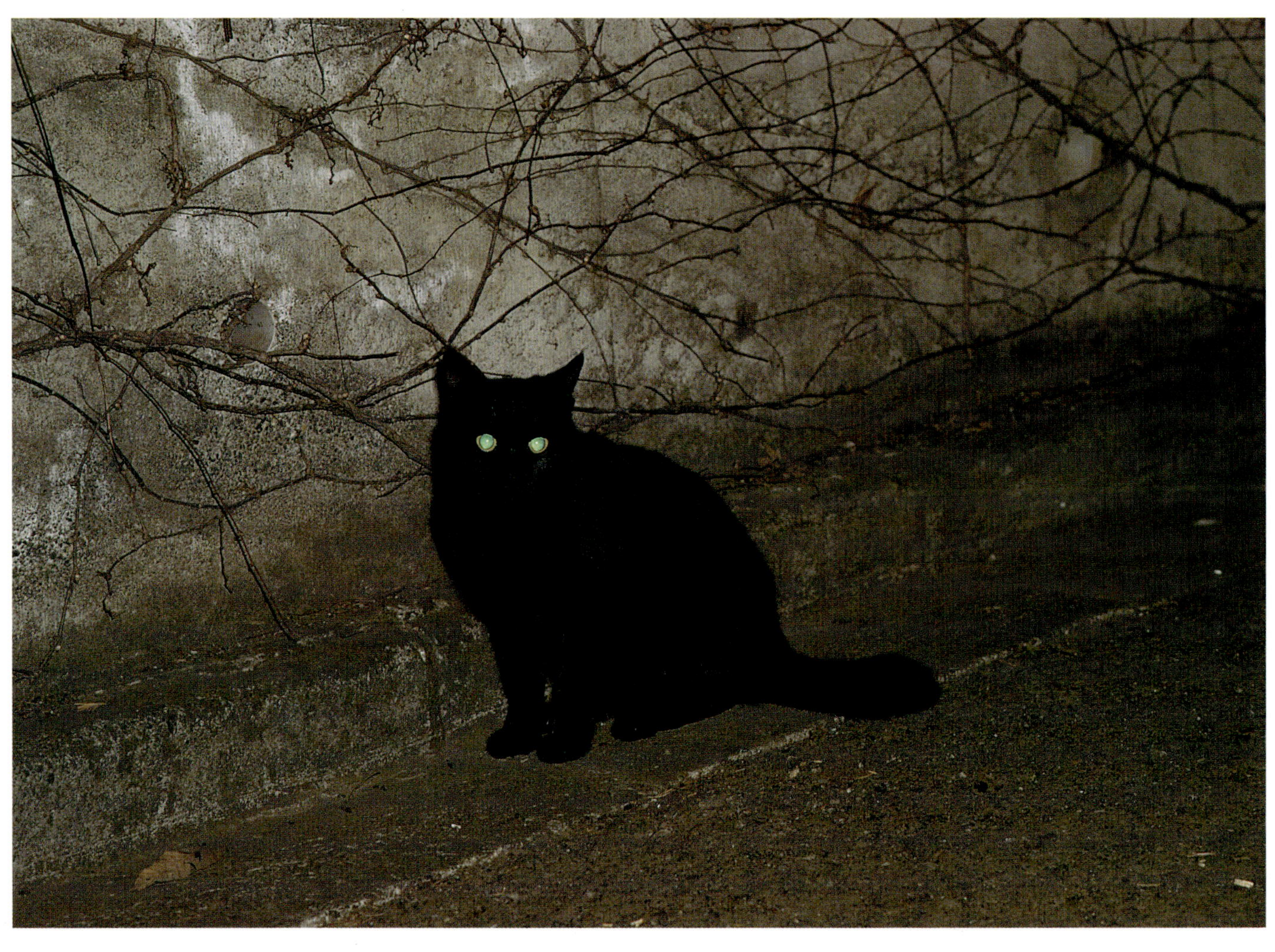

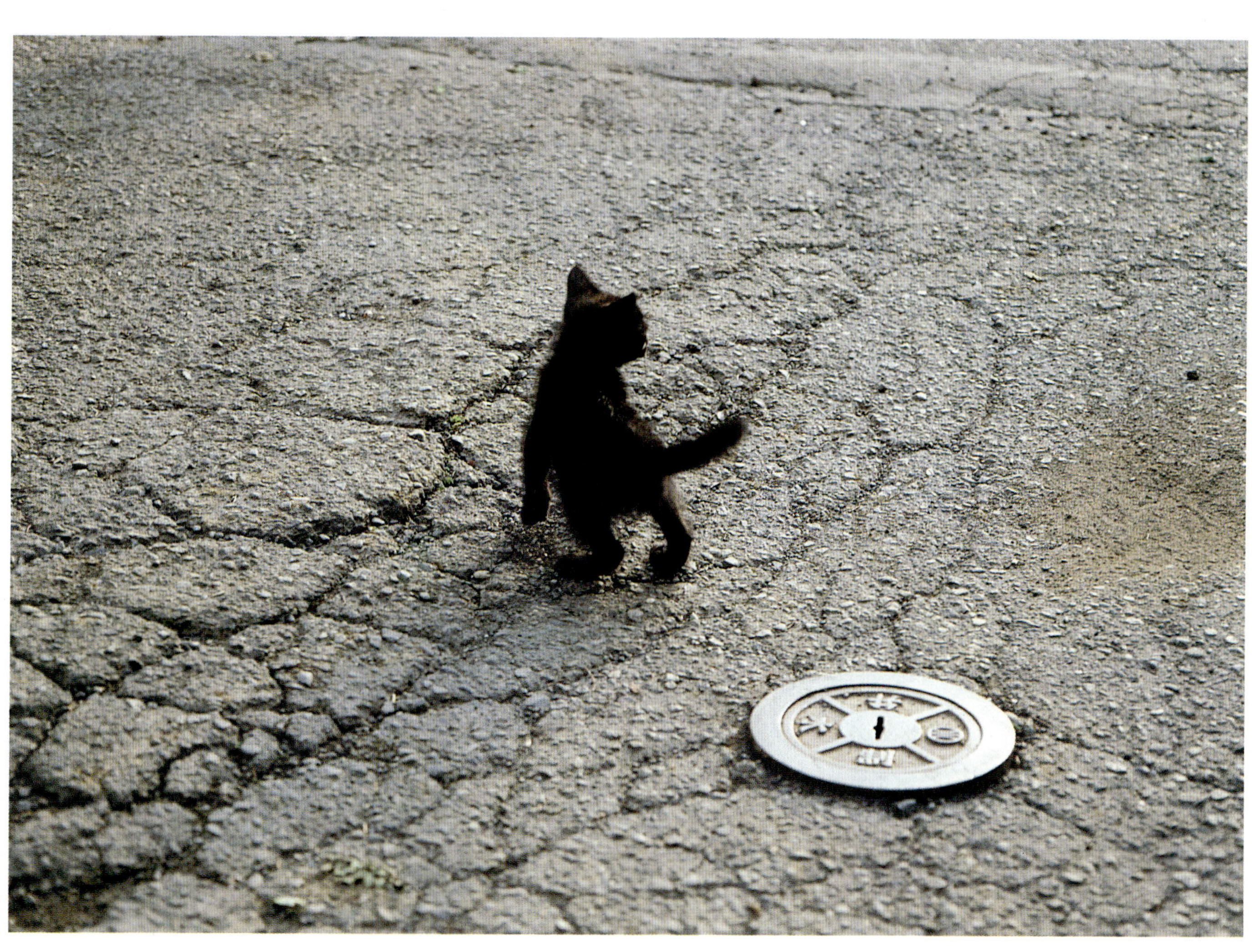

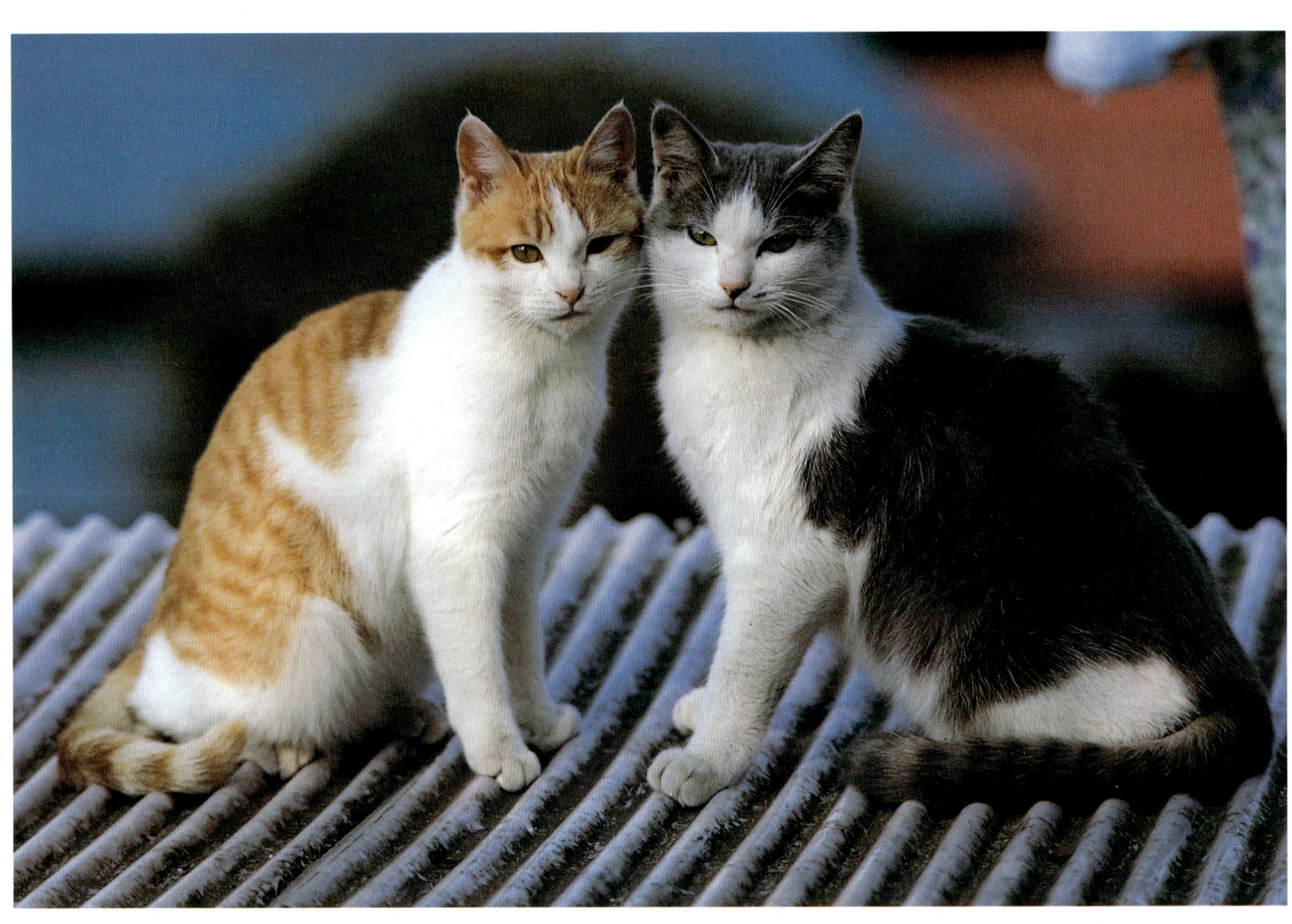

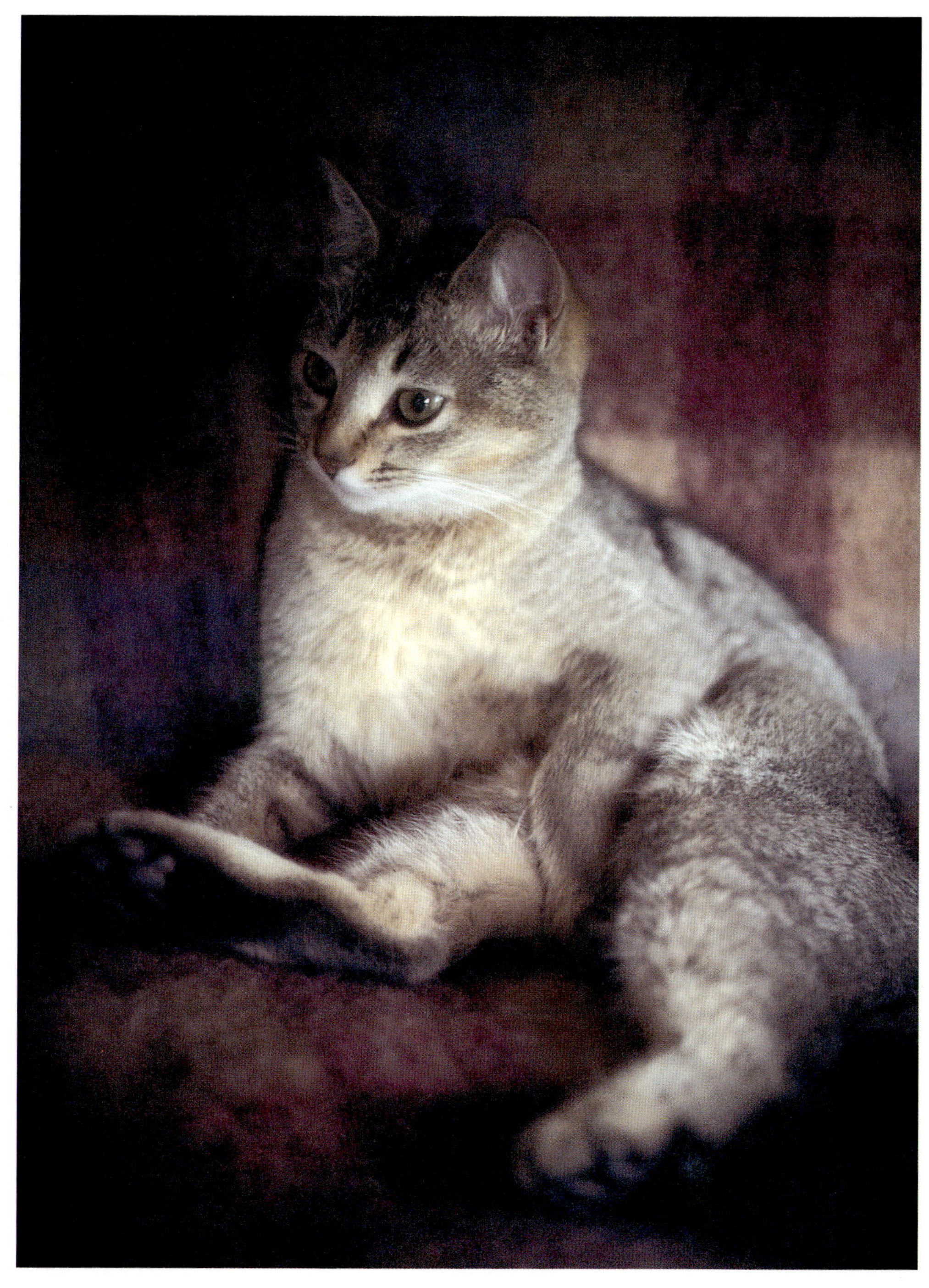

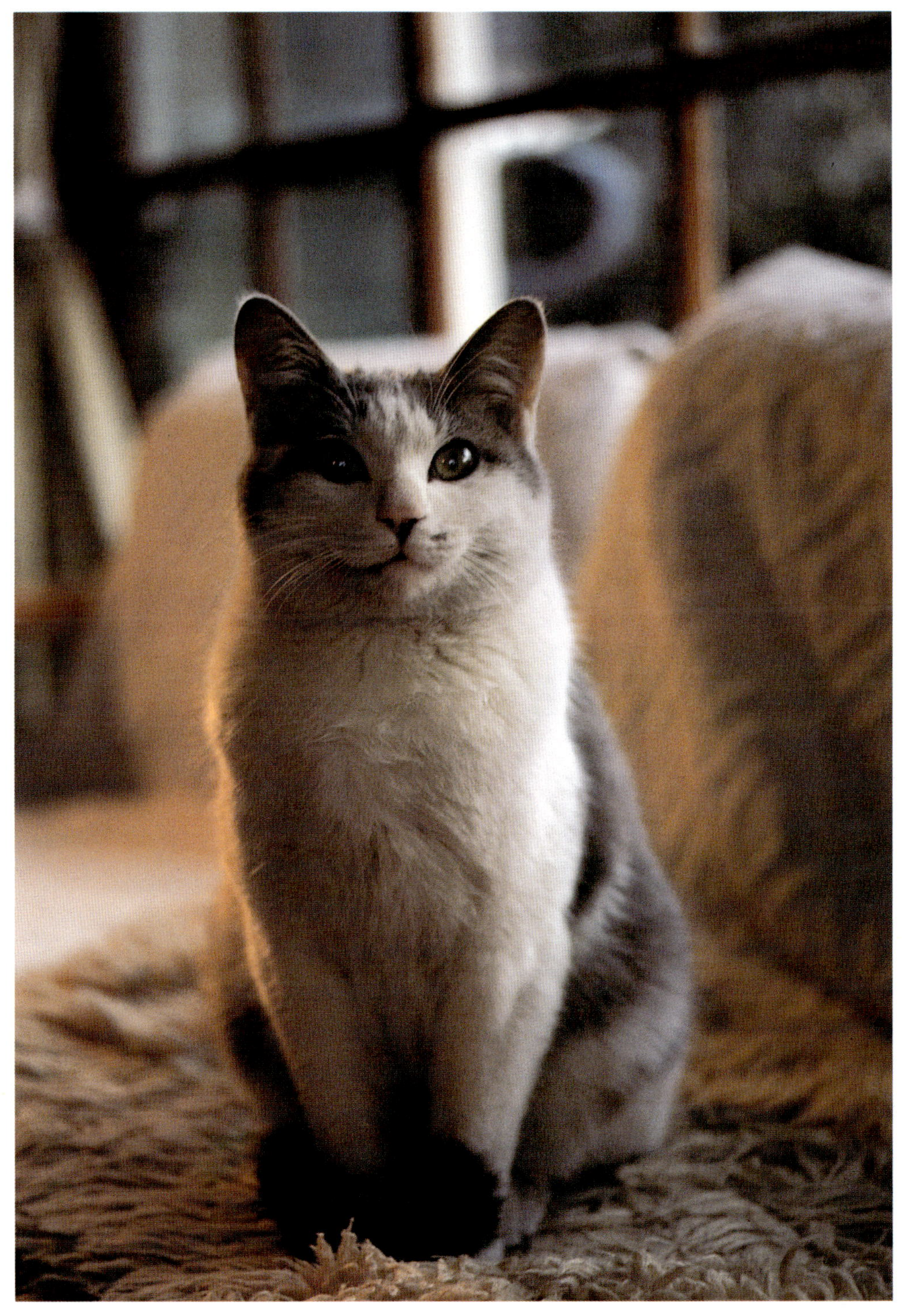

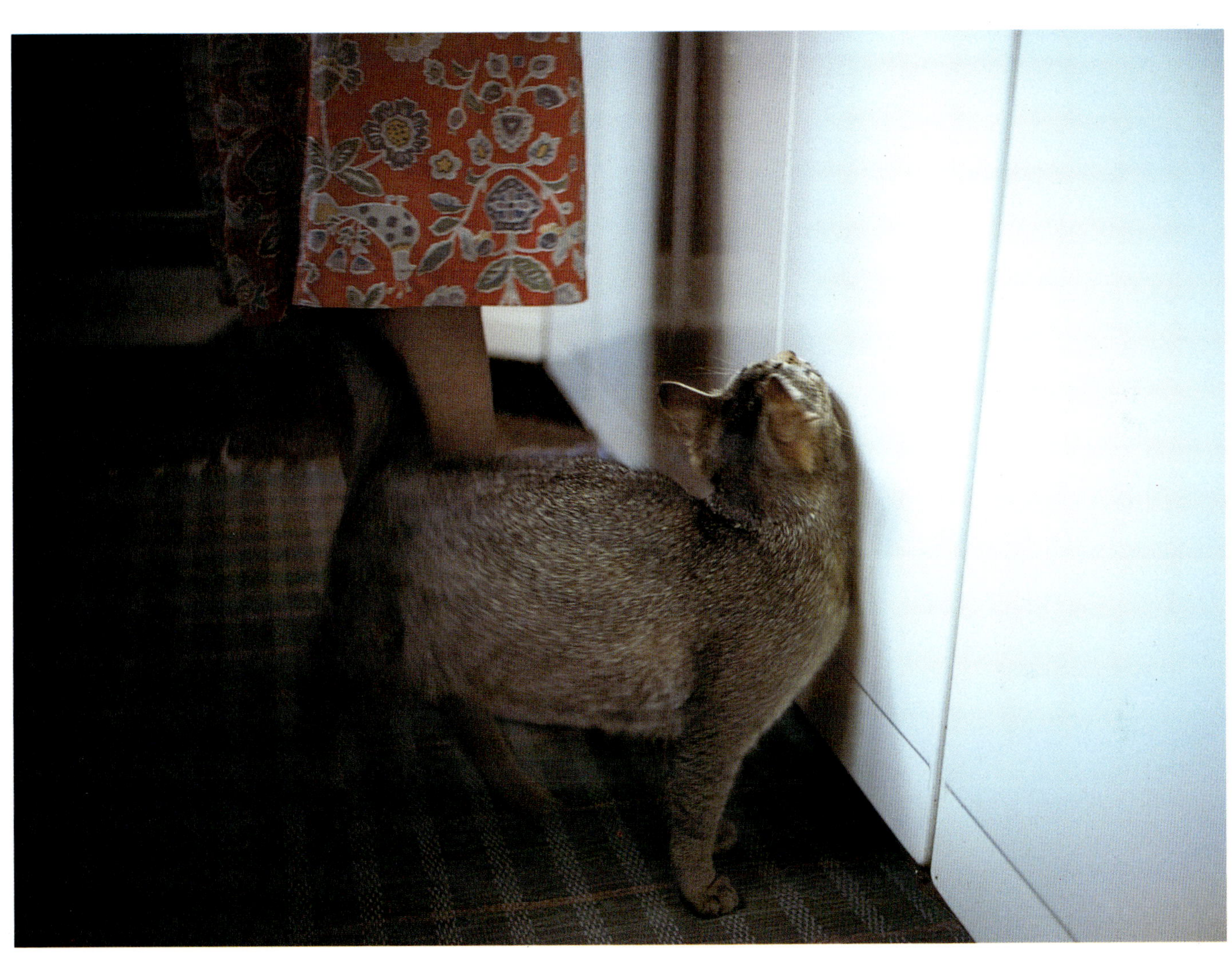

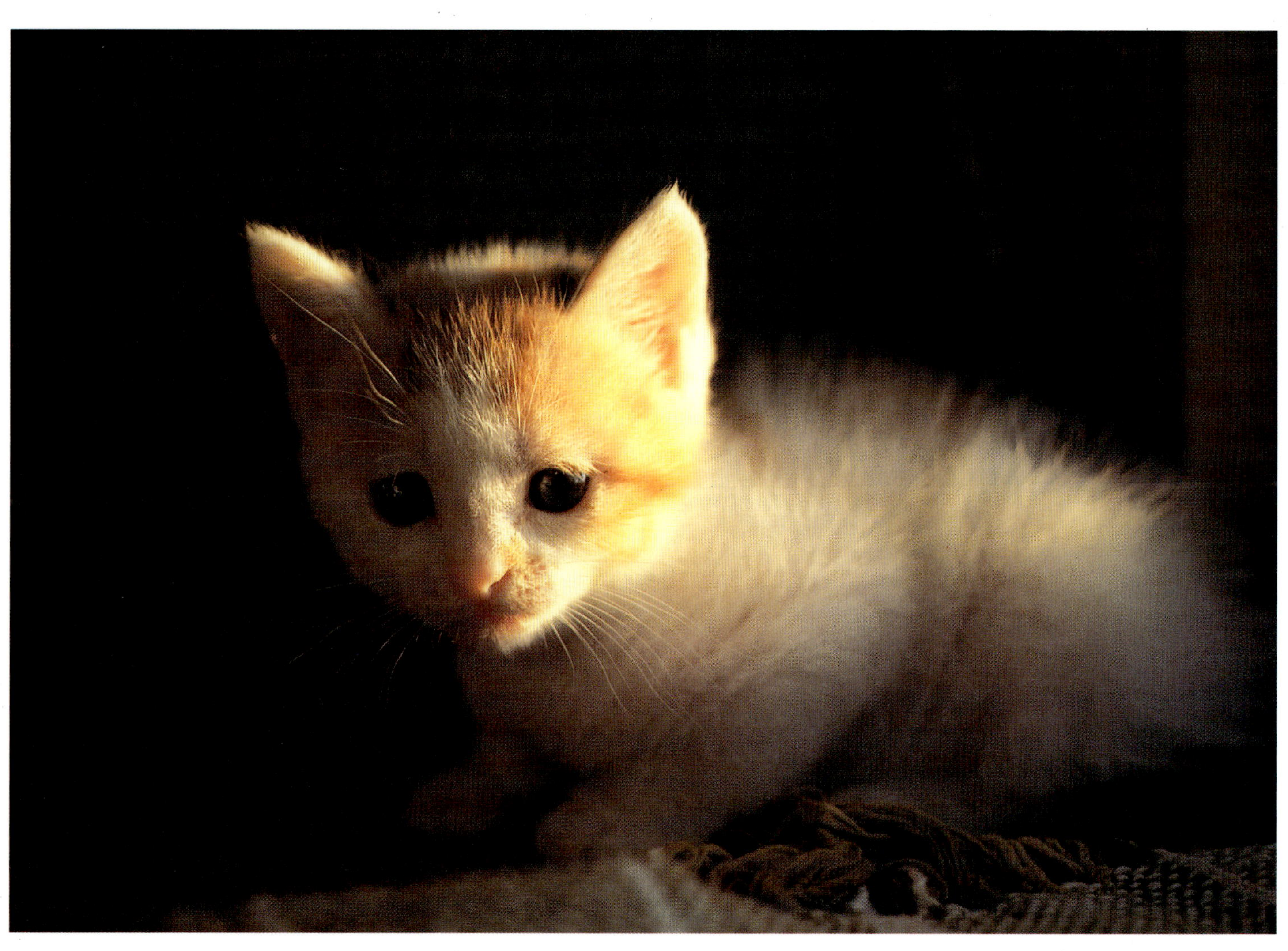

仔猫あげます

諏訪 優
詩人

不忍通りに平行したやや細い通りを，田端から谷中を経て，根津のあたりまでよく散歩する。正しくは愛染川を暗渠にして敷かれた谷田橋通り。常に燈明と一升ビンの絶えない延命地蔵のあたりは，そこだけ夜店通りと呼ばれ，決った日に夜店が並んだそうだが，今は名称だけが残っている。

谷中銀座を過ぎて根津までは，道はせばまり，左右にいくつもの路地があって，急に古い下町の風情になる。このあたりでやたらに逢うのが猫である。どれも人なつっこいから，飼い猫かそうでなくても，適当な保護を受けていそうに思える。おっとりしている上に毛並がいい。

最近は血統が混じり合う機会も多いとみえて，オヤ，と思う美猫にも出逢う。　昔ながらの駄菓子屋さんや雑貨屋さんがあるくらいで，たいていは大工さんや職人さんの家を思わせるいわゆるしもたや風。猫に対する人情も厚いのにちがいない。

フト，なつかしい匂いが流れてきた。

細い路地にそのまま接した畳屋さんがあって，年老いた職人さんが青畳に太い針を刺している。なつかしく思いながら，通りすがりにガラス戸を見ると，半紙の貼紙に“仔猫あげます”とあった。

もう何年もお目にかかったことのない貼紙で，墨の字も枯れていた。畳屋さんの奥のボール箱か何かの中で，かわいい仔猫が数匹，母猫にじゃれついているにちがいない。声をかけて，頂いてくるわけにはいかない現在のわたしだが，ほのぼのとした気持になって散歩をつづけた。

どの家の軒下にも，びっしりと鉢植えの植物がおいてあって，今は紫陽花と鉄線の紫や白の花が目を楽しませてくれる。

帰りに，まだ入ったことのない赤提燈にでも寄ってみようか。

今年も6月半ばのことである。

Please Take a Kitten

Yu Suwa
Poet

In the old part of Tokyo called Ueno, there is a certain rather narrow street which runs parallel to Shinobazudori Street. I often take a stroll along this street, starting from Tabata, passing through Yanaka and walking as far as Nezu. Properly speaking, this street is called Yatabashidori Street ; it was made by covering over a small river, the Aizengawa. At one point one comes across a wayside statue of Enmei Jizo, the popular bodhisattva of longevity, which is always surrounded by offerings of lamps and big sake bottles. This part is known as Yomisedori or Night Stall Street ; in the old days, so it is said, rows of night stalls were put out on certain fixed days. Now, however, only the name remains.

Between Yanaka Ginza and Nezu, the street narrows and a number of small lanes run off to the left and right. Suddenly one finds oneself breathing in the atmosphere of the old *shitamachi*, the traditional entertainment and shopping section of Tokyo. Around here one meets a lot of cats. All of them are friendly, so they must be either pet cats or, if not pets, then at least well looked after. Not only are they relaxed and gentle, but also their fur is glossy.

Recently, by the look of things, an increasing number of pedigree cats have been mixing with the natives, and sometimes one will encounter a really startlingly beautiful cat.

Around here, you can still find old-fashioned cheap sweet shops and grocery shops ; most of the houses are in the old *shimotaya* style and look like the homes of carpenters or other traditional artisans. Undoubtedly the people around here are very soft-hearted towards cats.

Suddenly a nostalgic fragrance strikes the nostrils.

There is a tatami-mat shop opening onto a narrow lane. In the shop, an old craftsman sits running a thick needle into the fresh rushes used for the matting. As I pass by, full of nostalgia, I happen to look up and see a piece of rice paper pasted onto the glass sliding door. It says : 'Please take a kitten'.

It is many years since I have seen this kind of notice ; even the ink in which it is written looks faded. No doubt, somewhere in the back of the shop, four or five kittens are playing with their mother in a cardboard box or the like. It is impossible for me in my present circumstances to call out and ask for a kitten. Yet, as I continue my stroll, I feel that I have seen something heartwarming.

Beneath the eaves of every house, there is a profusion of potted plants ; just now the eyes are greeted everywhere by the white and purple hydrangeas and clematis.

On the way home, I think to myself, perhaps I'll drop in for a drink somewhere new.

This happened around the middle of June this year.

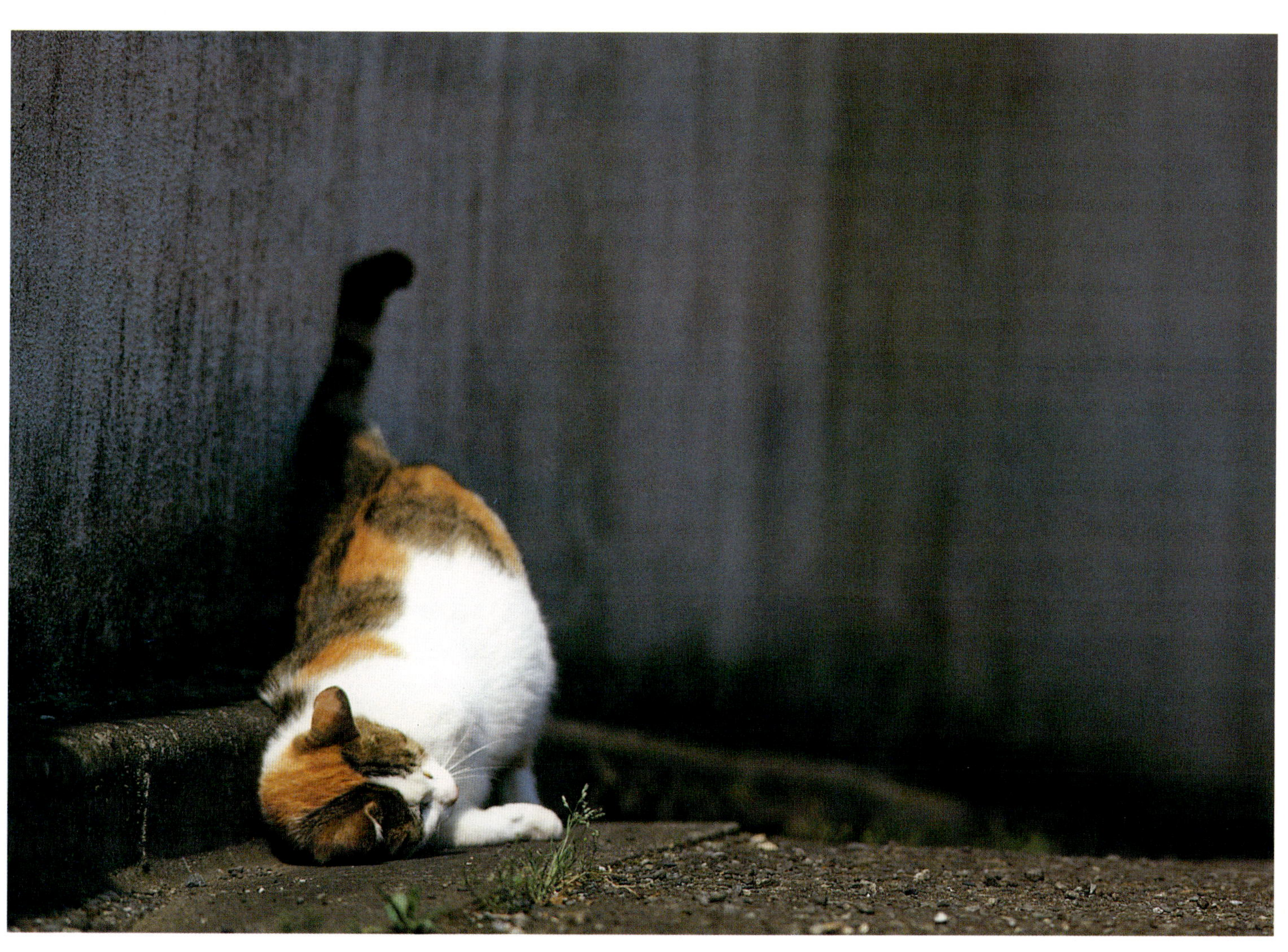

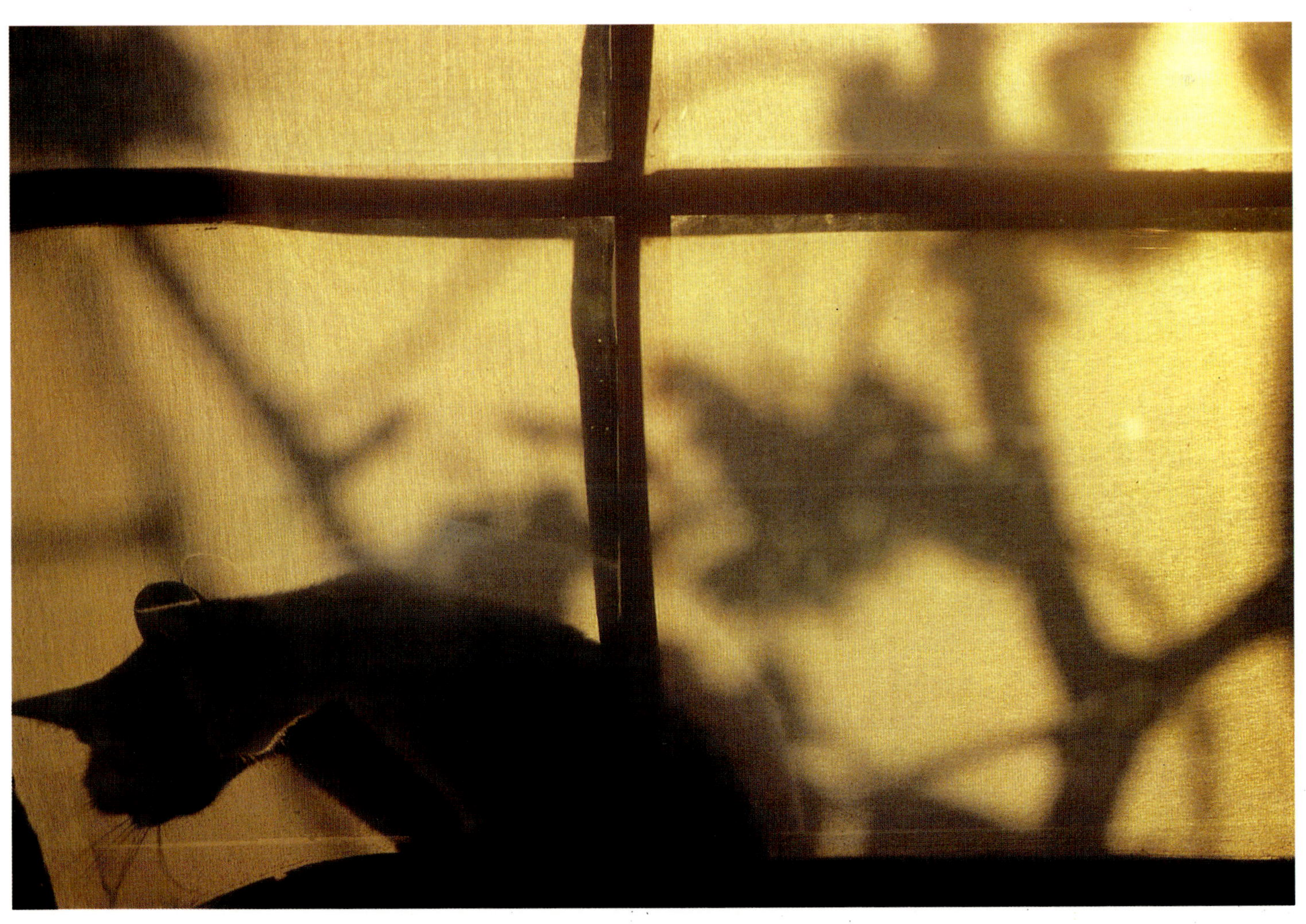

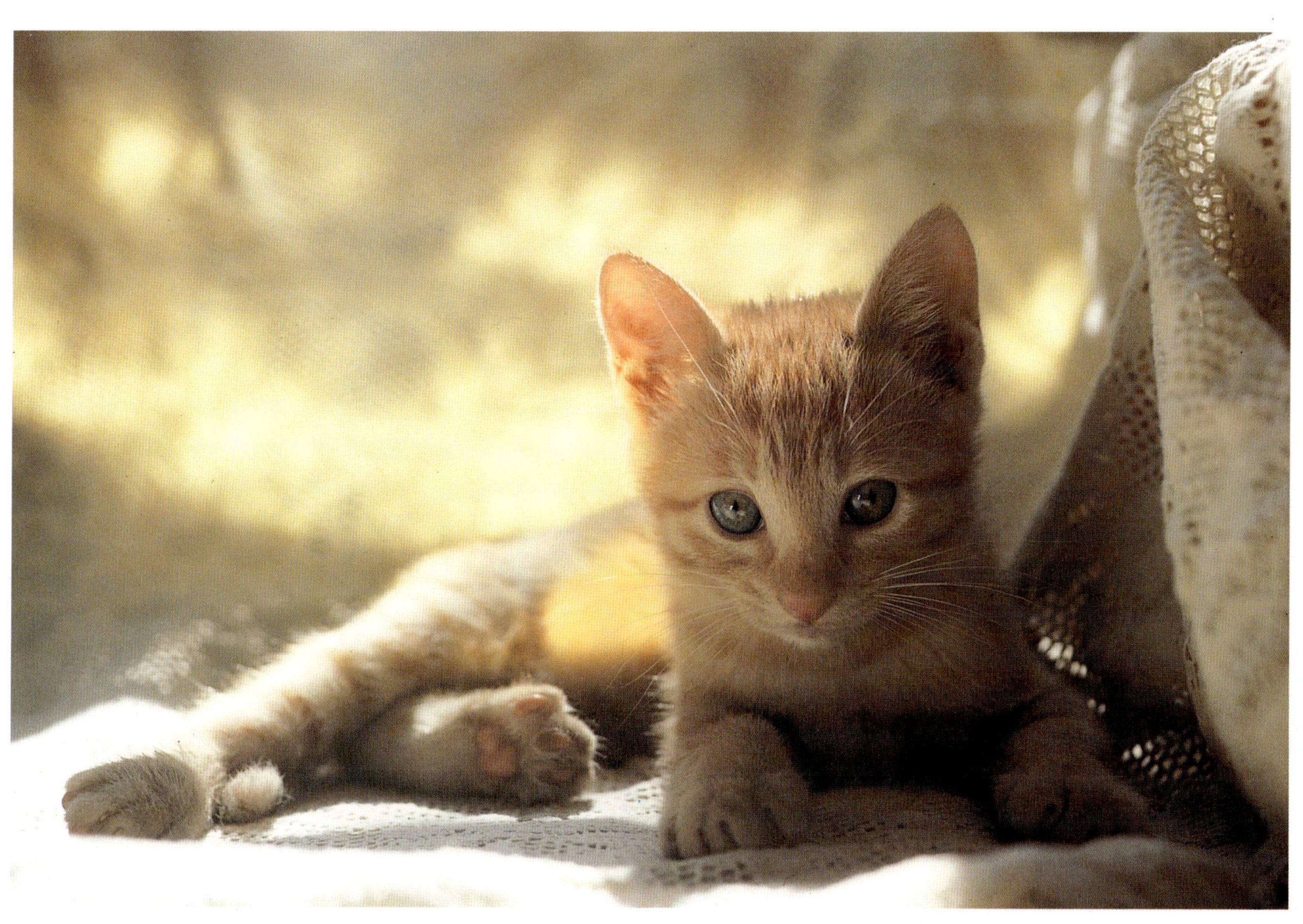

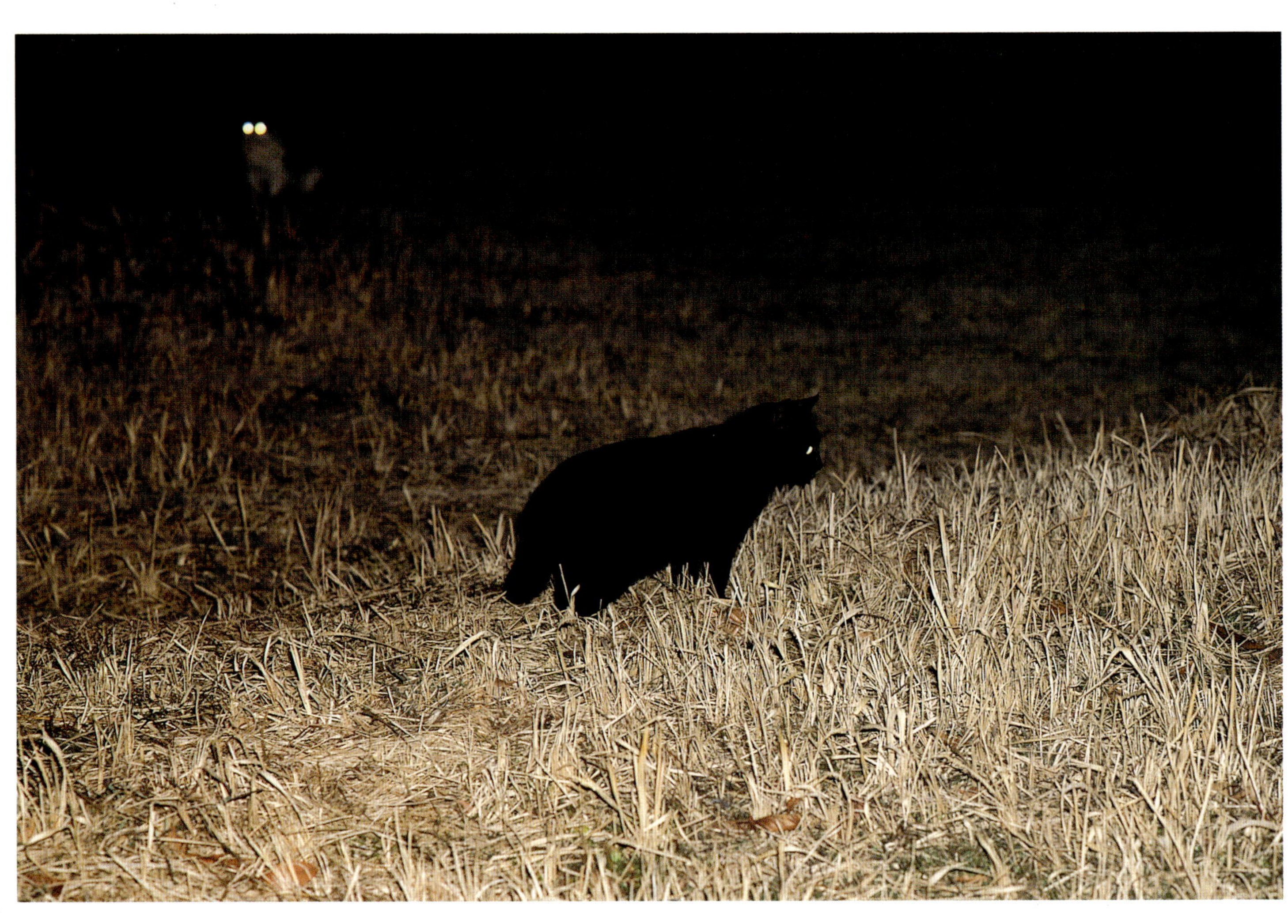

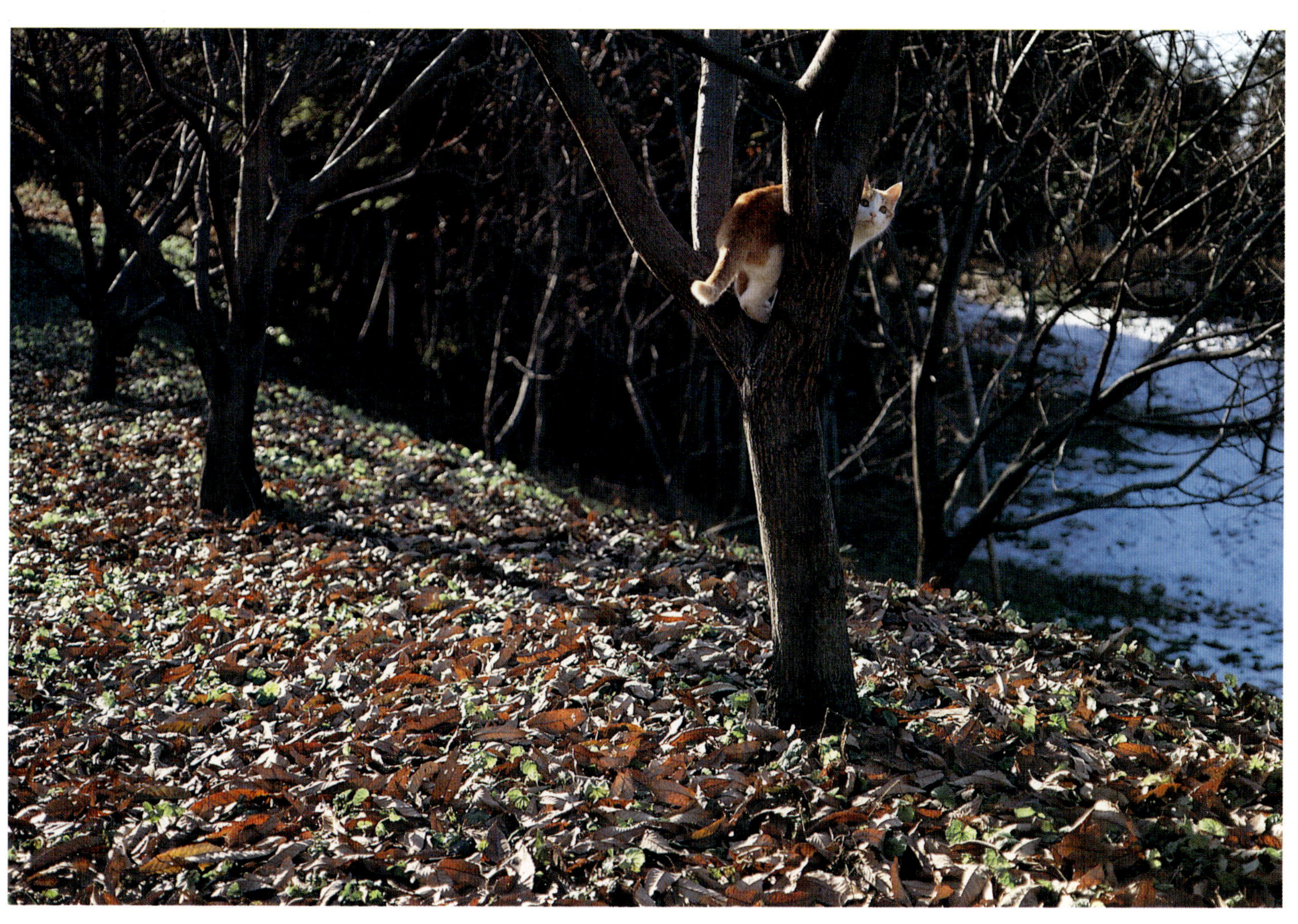

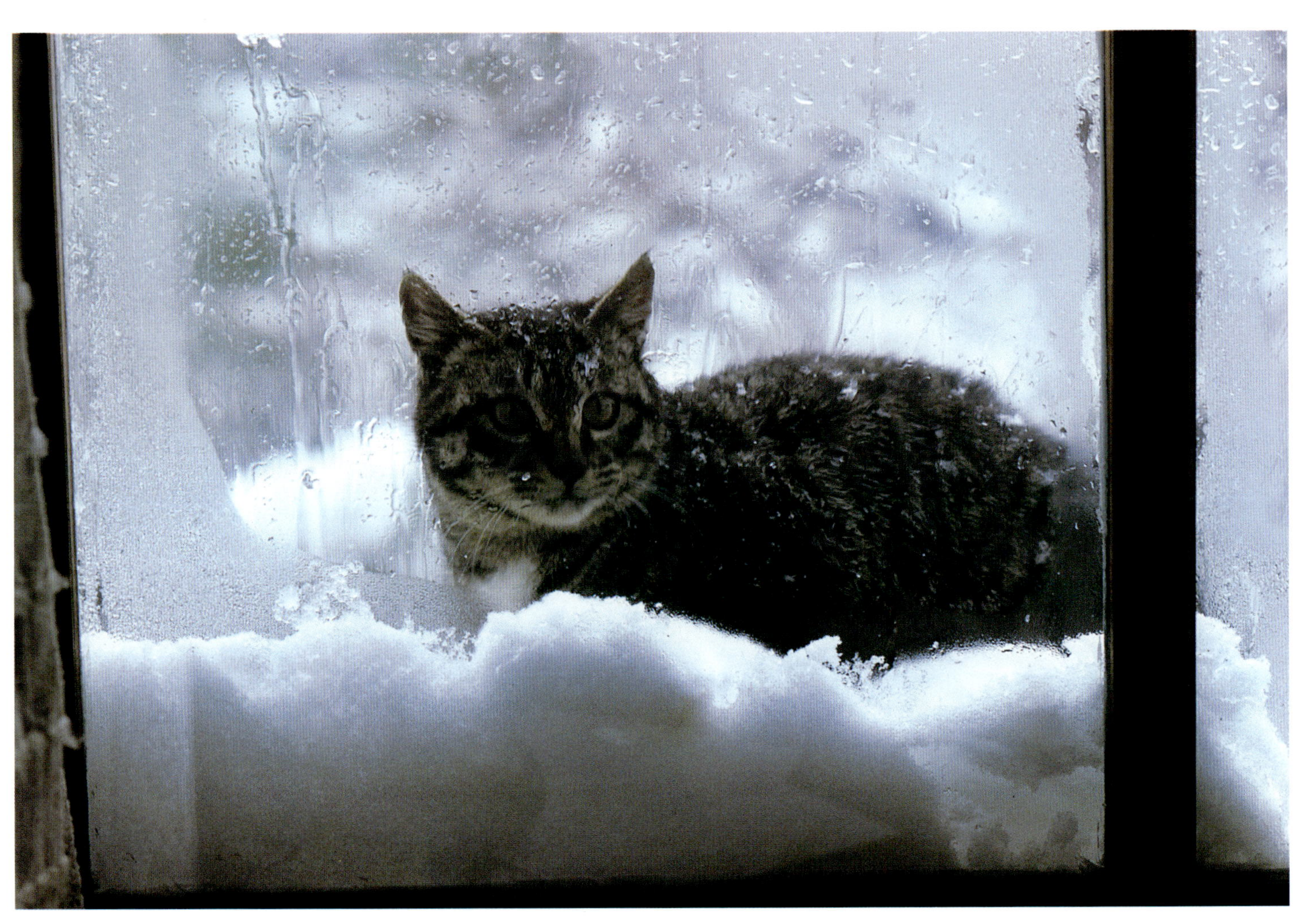

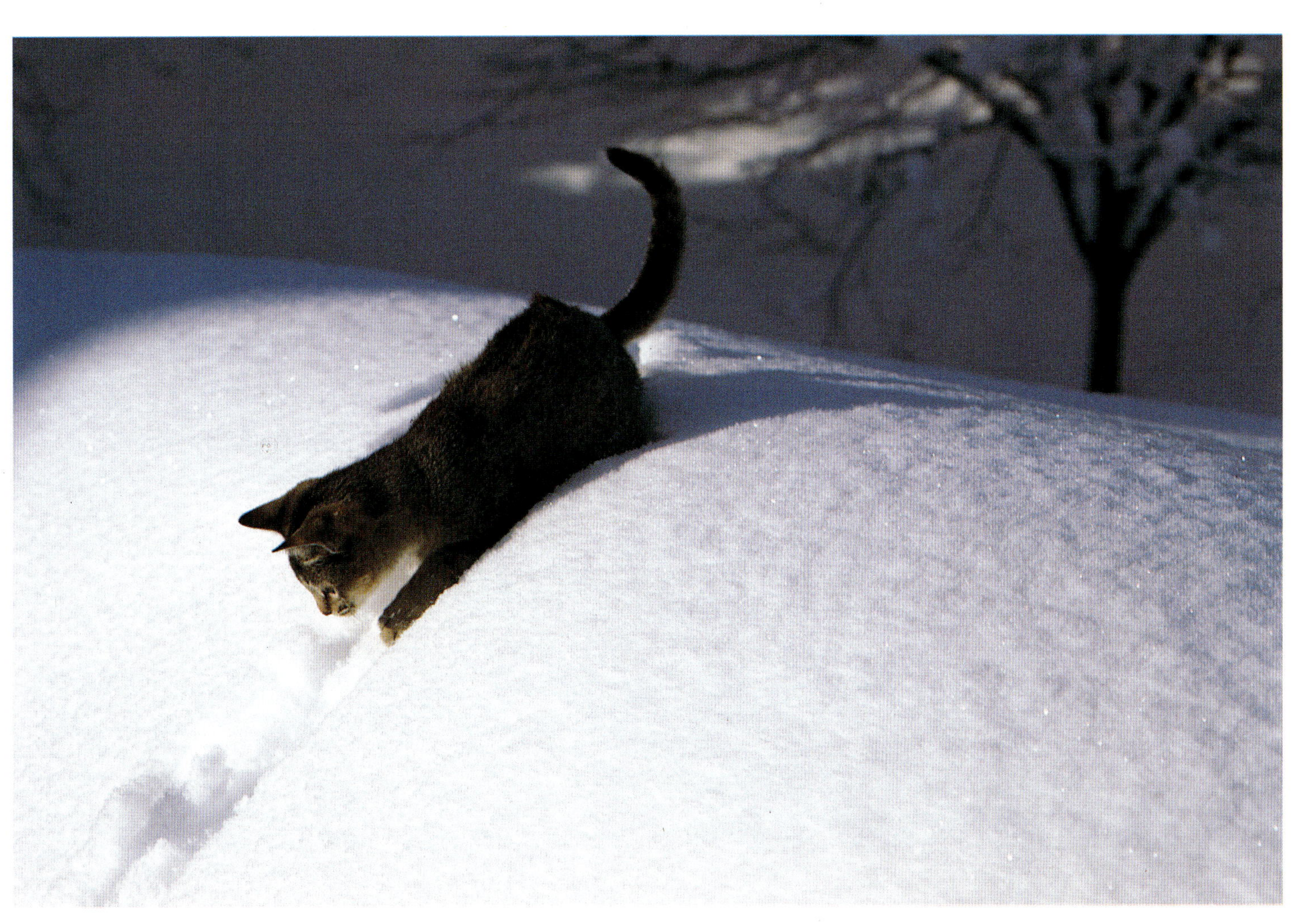

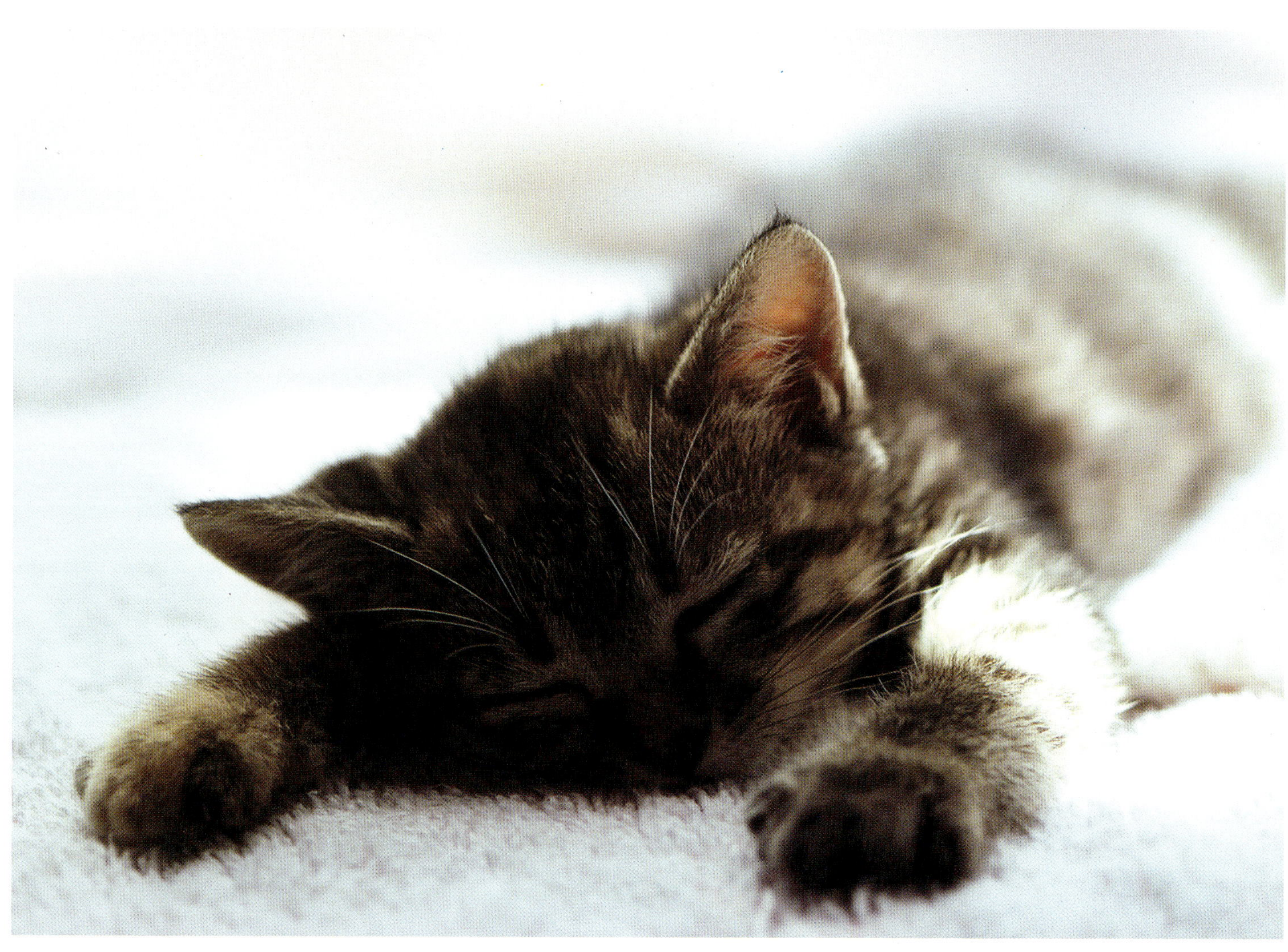

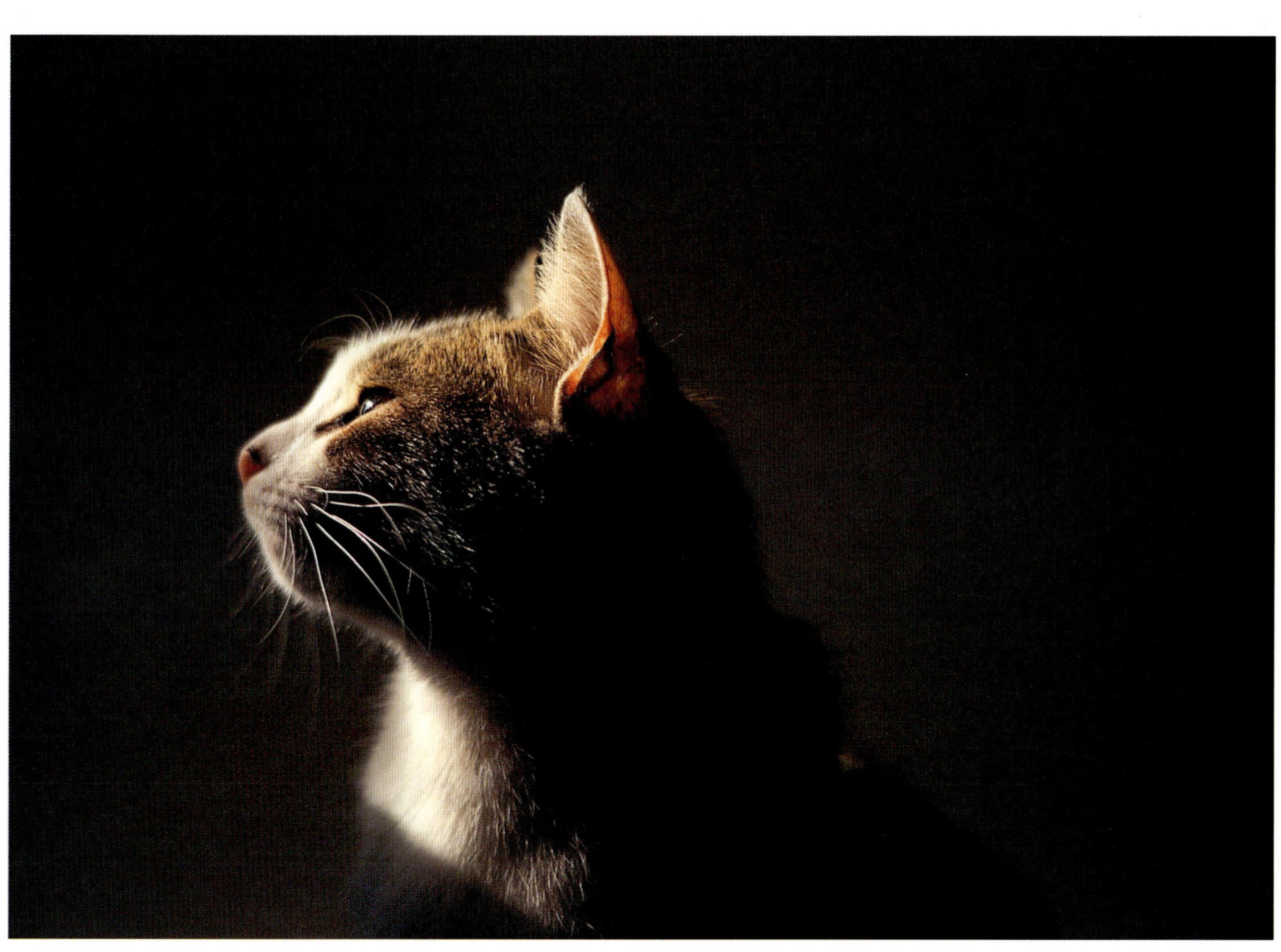

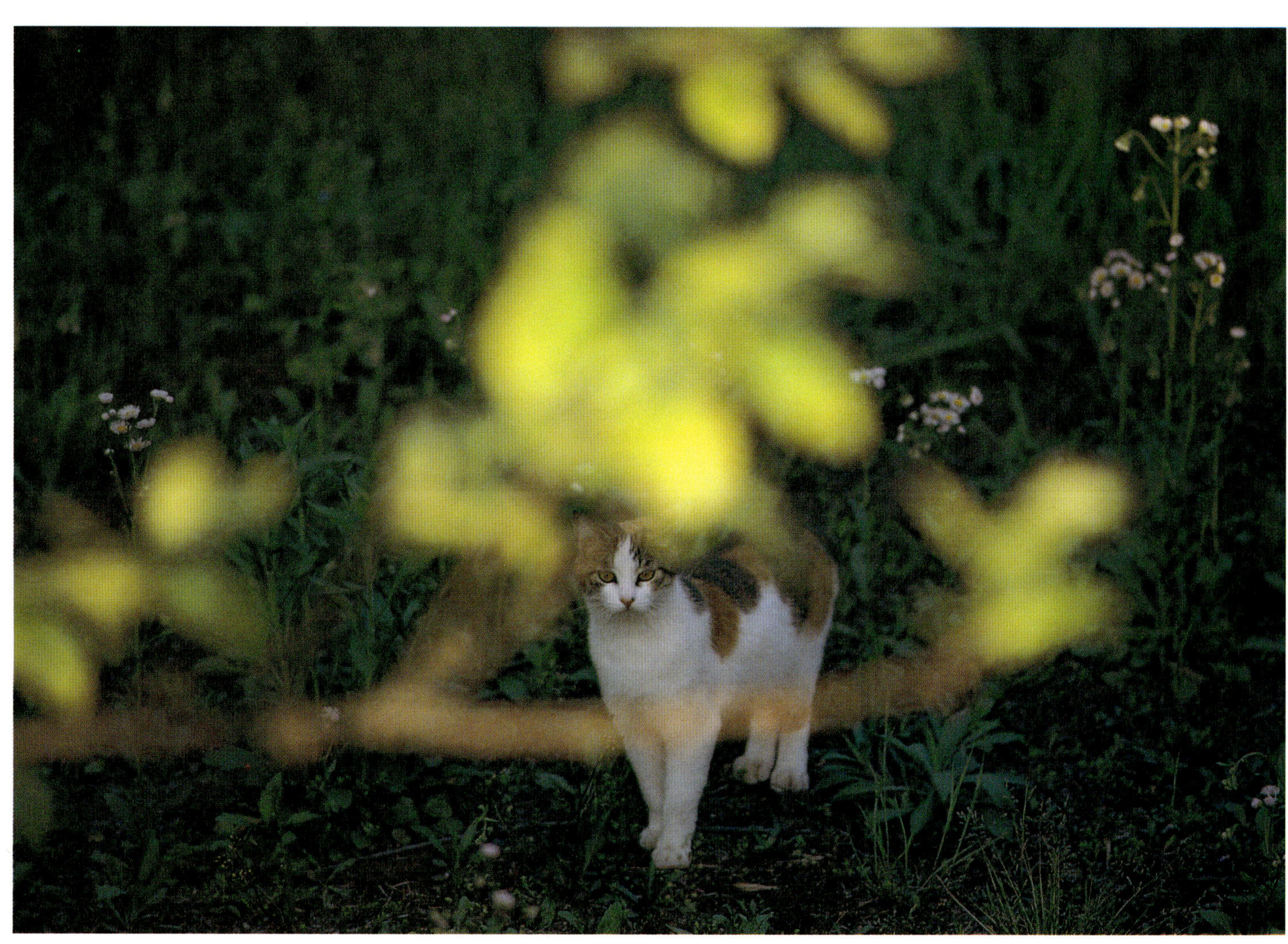

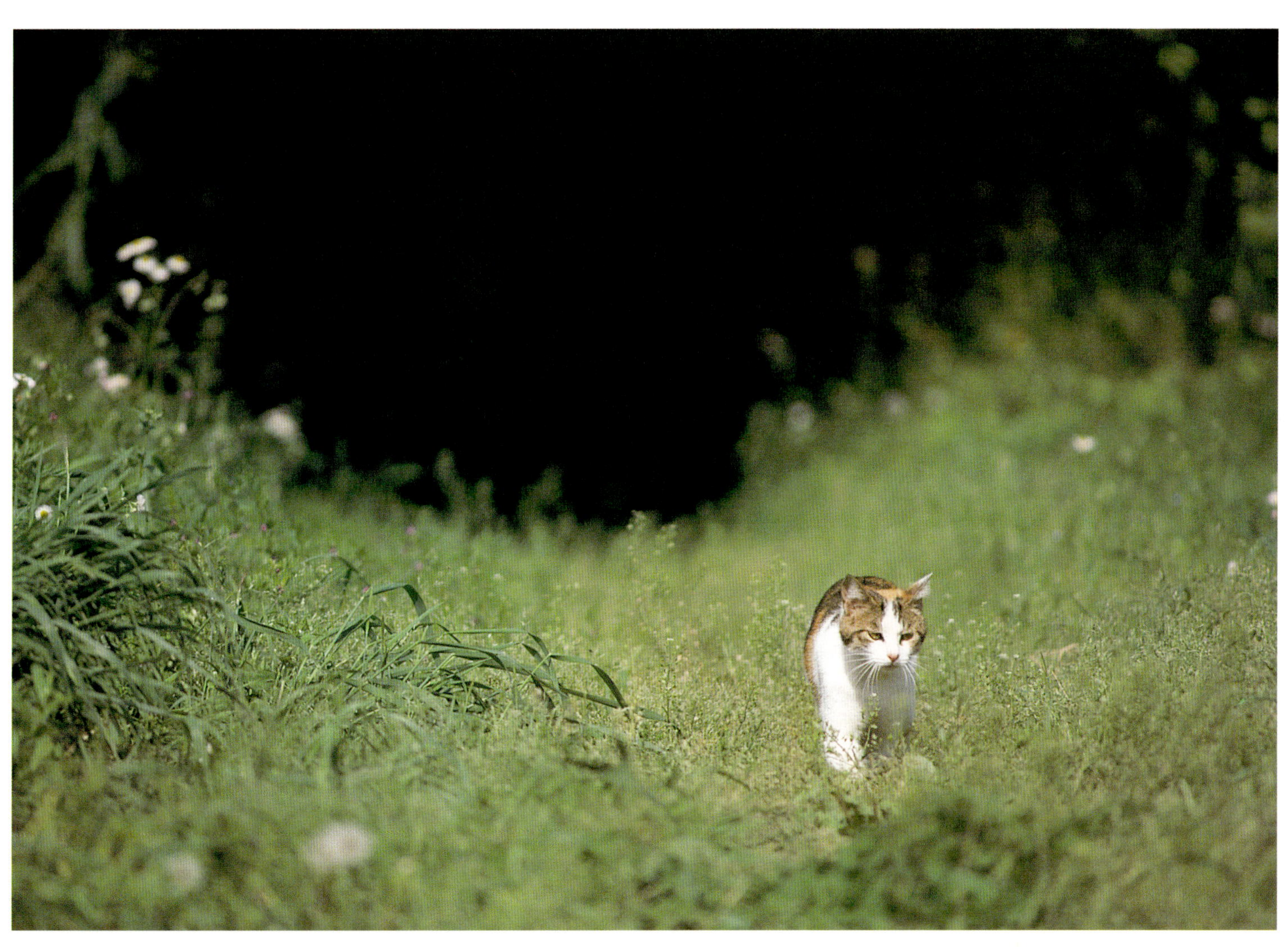

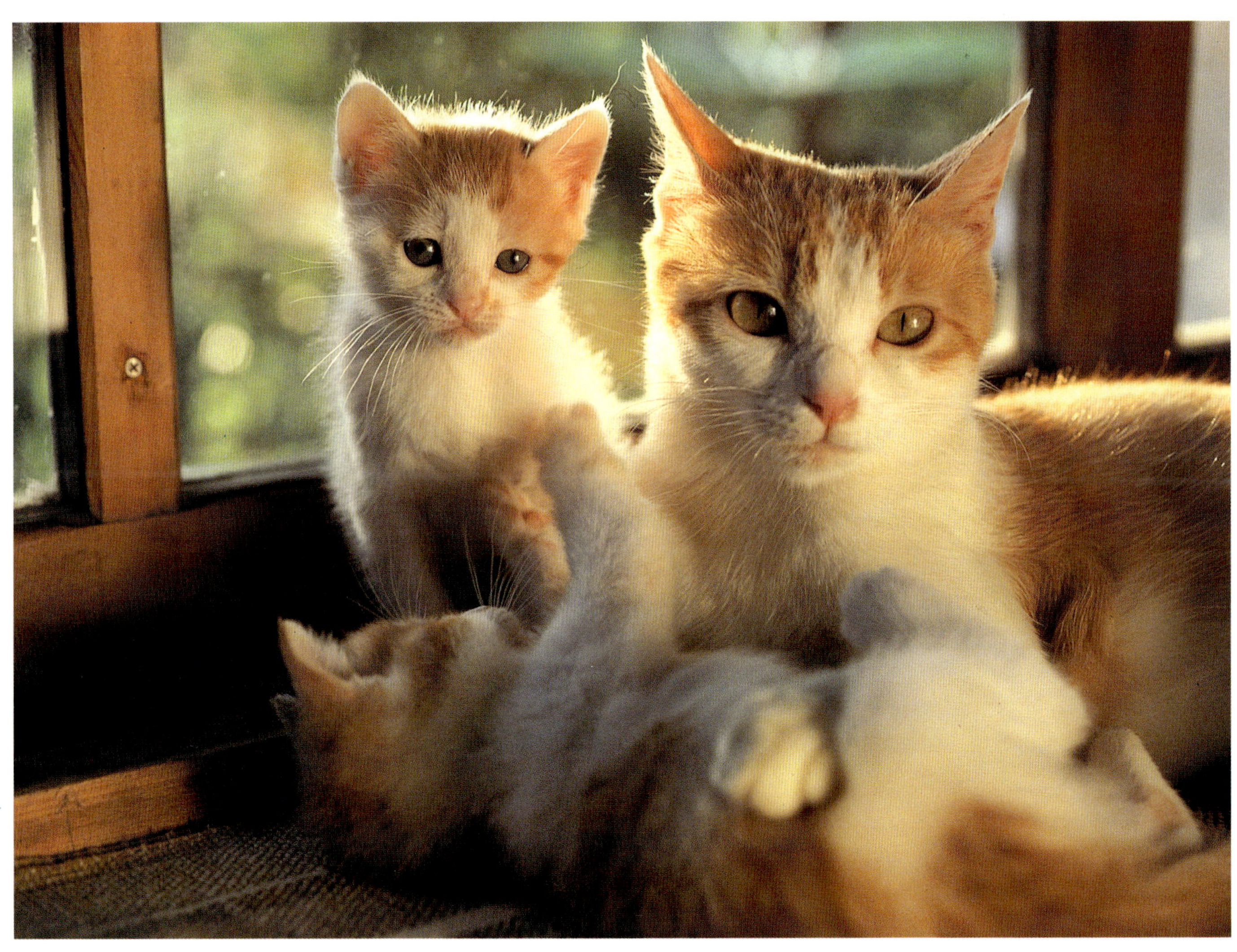

ポッポ	Poppo
モモコ	Momoko
キンタ	Kinta
ジェイ	Jay
ヨモ	Yomo
ヒメ	Hime
ジャック	Jack
ラビ	Rabi
チャーミィー	Charmey
ミケ	Mike
ブト	Buto

この写真集に登場した猫たちのわが家での呼び名です。その時々の，気まぐれな人間の気分で付けられた名がほとんどです。もちろん，猫たちの知ったことではないはずなのに，名付けられた雰囲気の猫に成長していくから不思議です。(山下)

These are the names which my family and I use for the cats which appear in this book. Most of them are names which we human beings arbitrarily gave the cats on the spur of thc moment.
Naturally the cats themselves cannot have been conscious of this, but to a mysterious degree they have all grown to suit their names. (T.Yamashita)

あとがき

猫たちと暮して，10年が過ぎようとしている。拾った猫，もらった猫，家で産まれた猫，もらわれていった猫，突然に家出した猫，病死した猫……。それぞれの猫たちに，濃淡の違いはあっても，鮮やかに蘇る固有の思い出がある。そうした猫たちを折にふれて写真に撮り始めて6年ほどになるだろうか。ふり返ってみると，写真を撮っているうちに，次第に猫の魅力にとり込まれていったように思う。

カバーの写真，「ポッポ」という猫のことだが，まさかカバーを飾るとは思っていなかった。公園の片隅に，バスタオルにくるまれ，かたわらにはぬいぐるみが添えられ，それとなく目立つように，つまり“大切に”捨てられていたのを，散歩中の知人が見つけ，わが家に持ち込まれた2匹のうちの1匹だ。

生後1週間前後だったろうか，みるからに弱々しく，かろうじて生きている，いや，生き延びることを期待させる材料はどこにも見いだせない，といった風だった。しかし，家の者一同で必死に面倒をみ，さらには，ちょうど授乳期にあった近所の母猫の乳房にしゃぶりつかせたりで，2匹とも苦難を乗り越えた。と書けば，よくある人と猫との美談の一つになるが，何よりも誉めあげるべきは，手の平にすっぽり収まるくらいの猫たちの，生きようとする意志であり，野生の強さであろう。1匹は親類にもらわれていって「桃子」。もう1匹がわが家で暮しているわけである。

ところでこのポッポ，アビシニアンに似ていると言われ，早速図鑑をめくる。似ている，クレオパトラがこよなく愛したという猫に。しかし決定的に何か違う。毛色だ。そうか，混血したから飼い主は捨ててしまったのだろうか。仮にそうだとしたら，悲しいことだ。混血でもいいではないか，猫は猫なのだ。「ポッポよ，普通が一番だよ！」と，ぼくは言いながらシャッターを切った……。

最後になりましたが，日高敏隆氏，諏訪優氏，川本三郎氏，佐野洋子氏，中沢けい氏には，お忙しいなか，素晴らしい文章を寄せていただき，本当に有難うございました。心から御礼を申し上げます。また，デザイナーの大塚あや子氏の細かい気配りとグラフィック社の奥田政喜氏のねばり強い情熱にも支えられて無事出版できましたこと，深く感謝しています。

山下寅彦

Afterword

It is nearly ten years since I began to share my home with cats. Amongst these cats there have been some which we have found on the streets, some which we have been given, some which have been born in our home, some which we have given away, some which have upped and left us, some which have died from illness..... Each of these cats, despite their rich variety, has left us with vivid memories. I started to take photographs of the cats about six years ago. Looking back, I realise that it was the process of taking the photographs which gradually opened my eyes to their true charm.

On the cover of this book there appears a photograph of a cat called Poppo. Actually I never dreamt that this cat would appear on the jacket of a book! It was one of two which an acquaintance of mine found in the corner of a park and brought to our house. The two cats were wrapped in a bathtowel and had a soft toy placed next to them ; one got the impression that whoever had abandoned them had done so with 'love'.

They were at that time only about a week old. They looked so weak that they seemed barely alive. In fact, it did not look as though they had any real chance of surviving. However, the whole family devoted themselves to looking after the kittens. There was a local cat who happened at that time to be suckling her young and we put the two kittens to her breast. Somehow they recovered and survived. Written down like this, it sounds rather like yet another moral tale of human kindness to cats, but actually what really deserves our admiration is the will to live, the natural animal strength, of these two kittens, each tiny enough to fit snugly into the palm of one hand. One of the kittens was taken in by relatives and is called Momoko. The other lives with us.

Incidentally, I was once told that Poppo looks like an Abyssinian cat and I immediately looked up the breed in an illustrated reference book. Sure enough there was a resemblance between Poppo and the cat that is said to have been doted on by Cleopatra. At the same time, however, there was also something different. It was the colour of the fur. I realised that Poppo must have been abandoned by its owner because it was not a pure Abyssinian but had some other blood as well. If this was the case, then it struck me as rather sad. Surely a cat is a cat, whether it is pedigree or not. "Poppo, it's best to be ordinary!" I would call encouragingly as I clicked the shutter.

Last of all, I would like to take this opportunity to thank Toshitaka Hidaka, Yu Suwa, Saburo Kawamoto, Yoko Sano and Kei Nakazawa, who, despite being extremely busy, provided such splendid essays for this collection. I am deeply grateful to them. I would also like to express my deep gratitude to Ayako Otsuka, the designer of the book, for all her careful thought and Seiki Okuda of Graphic-sha Publishing Company for his unwavering enthusiasm for the project. Without their support the book could never have been brought safely to publication.

Torahiko Yamashita

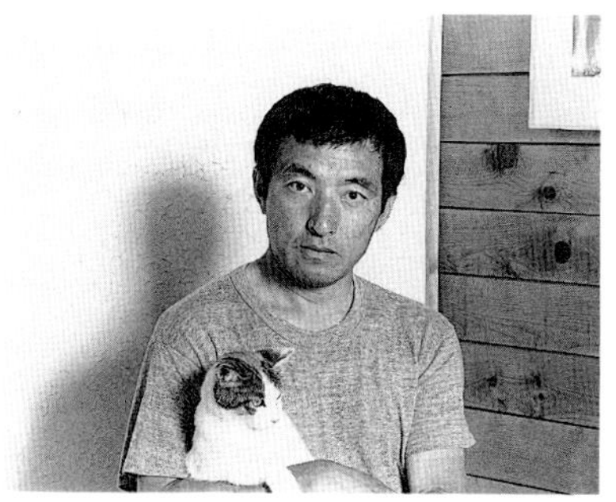

山下寅彦

写真家。宮崎県生まれ。
1972年，銀座ニコンサロンで個展「アノニム，アノニム」。
主に，エディトリアルの分野で活躍中。
写真集に，バラエティ・ムック「猫」(朝日新聞社)，
「ねこ・ネコ・子猫 パート３」(日本出版社)がある。

事務所:
107 東京都港区赤坂9-6-28 アルベルゴ乃木坂1101
TEL03-404-9518
スタジオ:
194-02 東京都町田市上小山田町39-2
TEL0427-97-3381

❑

レイアウト/カバーデザイン:
大塚あや子
翻訳:
エイドリアン・J・ピニングトン

❑

Torahiko Yamashita

Photographer
Born in Miyazaki Perfecture, Japan.
Held his first one-man exhibition ‘Anonym, Anonym’ at the Nikon Salon in Ginza in 1972.
Chiefly active in the editorial field.
He has previously published two books of cat photographs, ‘Variety Mook : Neko’ (Asahi Shimbunsha) and ‘Neko, Neko, Koneko : Part III’ (Nihon Shuppansha).

Office :
Room 1101, Albergo Nogizaka, 9-6-28 Akasaka,
Minato-ku, Tokyo 107, Japan
Tel. 03-404-9518
Studio :
39-2 Kamioyamada-cho, Machida-shi,
Tokyo 194-02, Japan
Tel. 0427-97-3381

Layout/Cover design : Ayako Otsuka
English Translation : Adrian J. Pinnington

猫
CAT DAYS

1990年９月25日 初版第１刷発行

著者:
山下寅彦©
発行者:
久世利郎
印刷所:
凸版印刷株式会社
製本所:
和田製本株式会社
写植:
三和写真工芸株式会社
発行所:
株式会社グラフィック社
〒102 東京都千代田区九段北1-9-12
電話03-263-4318 振替 東京3-114345

ISBN4-7661-0573-7 C0072 P2600E